Inventors and Inventions

Creative Cross-Curricular Activities
• Fascinating Background Information
• Problem-Solving Investigations for All Students

by Lorraine Hopping Egan

S C H O L A S T I C
PROFESSIONAL BOOKS

New York ♦ Toronto ♦ London ♦ Auckland ♦ Sydney

Acknowledgments

The author is mightily grateful for the selfless and invaluable contributions of Louise Spigarelli, social studies teacher, St. Mel's Elementary School in Dearborn Heights, Michigan.

Design by Ellen Matlach Hassell
for Boultinghouse & Boultinghouse, Inc.

Illustration Credits Delana Bettoli, Antonio Castro,
Michael Moran, and Manuel Rivera

Photo research by Joan Beard and Ellen Matlach Hassell

Photo Credits Cover: Inventors & Inventions Cover photo credits
Ada Lovelace: Culver Pictures; sandwich: © FoodPix; girl and cereal: © David Waitz; old-time bicyclist: Corbis-Bettman; modern bicyclist: © Geisser/H. Armstrong Roberts; Thomas Edison: Brown Brothers/ Everett Collection
Interior: pp. 7, 8, 9: © PhotoDisc, Inc.;
p. 59: Taurus, courtesy Ford Motor Company

ISBN: 0-590-10388-1

Contents

Introduction

Imagine a day without inventions. Abandon your home, its contents, and all packaged, prepared, or cultivated foods. Then step into nature without even a spear for hunting. Few of us would last an hour—let alone 24 hours. Unlike every other animal on Earth, we humans depend on our inventions for survival. Inventions are our life-support systems.

Because inventions are so vital and so pervasive, a theme unit on the topic easily spans the school curriculum. *Inventors and Inventions* provides creative activities, ready-to-use materials, and a timeline game to cover concepts in social studies, math, science, language arts, and art. All activities include fascinating background information, lesson ideas, and extensions for scaling the material up or down. And sprinkled throughout the book, you'll find provocative quotes from inventors throughout history, along with ideas for using each quote as a basis for an instant lesson.

The first section of the book, "What's an Invention?" defines inventions and explores accidental inventions, inventions inspired by nature, science fiction inventions that came true, and more.

"Inventions Past, Present, and Future" and the interactive poster, "The Great All-Time Inventions Game," examine the effects of inventions on American and world history. Students research and create trading cards about famous and not-so-famous inventors, interview senior citizens, and use science to distinguish fraudulent inventions from real ones and make an accurate water clock. Since inventions make our lives better, a math activity about transportation asks, "How much better?"

In "Inventive Thinking and Creating," students become inventors. The section includes high-level thinking exercises, hands-on science activities, problem-solving challenges, market surveys, cost calculations, and practice in reading and writing patents.

Maurine Marchani, a seventh-grade teacher who has inspired and guided many successful young inventors, believes that childhood is the perfect time to be an inventor: "Nobody has told seventh graders they aren't creative yet." The projects in *Inventors and Inventions* aim to keep it that way.

—*Lorraine Hopping Egan*

What's an Invention?

The word invention evokes images of fancy contraptions and devices, wacky gizmos and gadgets. But most inventions are ordinary parts of our everyday lives—a new garden rake, can opener, or car model, for example. And many inventions aren't contraptions at all. The Toll House™ recipe for chocolate chip cookies is one tasty example.

An invention is any new thing that makes something faster, easier, more powerful, more efficient, more attractive, more accurate, more fun, or more productive—in short, just plain better.

In this section, students will identify and discuss inventions, distinguish inventions (creations) from discoveries (things that already exist), learn about accidental inventions and inventions inspired by nature, analyze bicycle designs, classify inventions as either science fiction or science fact, and debate the delicate question of who owns a patent for an expensive cancer cure.

I Spy an Invention

Students classify inventions and noninventions.

Curriculum
Connections
✓ Social Studies
✓ Language Arts
✓ Science

Background

The original Latin meaning of the word *invent* is to "come upon or find." But you can come upon a chair and still not invent it. A better definition might be to "concoct, devise, or create."

Above all else, an invention must be new—either something that someone created or a new use for something old. For example, the technique of finger painting didn't exist until it was invented in the 1920s. Engineer Auguste Bartholdi won a patent (No. 11,023) for his original design of the Statue of Liberty on February 18, 1879. A new variety of apple, the sport of mountain biking, and the latest toy fad are all examples of inventions,

Lesson Ideas

Invite students to look around the classroom for inventions (almost any human-made object, including a hybrid plant). As an added challenge, tell them that their goal is to find and write down inventions that aren't on any-one else's list. After a few minutes, compare and discuss the items. Are any of the items not inventions? Why? In what way is each invention an improvement? Does it make something faster, easier, better, more attractive, or more fun? Hand out reproducible page 8 and ask students to consider which things on the list are inventions and which are not.

Answers

The only noninventions on the worksheet are electricity, fire, Pikes Peak, and moon rocks. Electrical power—turning electricity into usable energy—is definitely an invention. Can students explain the difference? Why is Mount Rushmore—the mountainside monument to presidents—an invention, but the mountain Pikes Peak isn't? *(Inventions are created by humans.)*

💡 **Extension**

Have students write an essay on the topic "Does every invention have to have an inventor?" Inventions such as languages have a continuous stream of inventors, usually unknown. Great artwork often has one obvious inventor. But what about artwork created by zoo elephants or primates? (A few zoos sell animal artwork to raise funds.) Can animals ever be inventors? Discuss tool-using chimpanzees, who use sticks to extract insects from logs.

"My favorite invention is always the next one."
—Bob Gundlach

WRITE: Gundlach invented the photocopier. What will the photo-copier of the future look like and be able to do?

I Spy an Invention

Read the list. Then put a check next to each thing that you think is _not_ an invention.

- ☐ Video games
- ☐ Electricity
- ☐ The alphabet
- ☐ The Spanish language
- ☐ Forest fires
- ☐ Matches
- ☐ A recipe for chocolate chip cookies
- ☐ A recipe for a cola drink
- ☐ The sport of basketball
- ☐ Sneakers
- ☐ The song "Happy Birthday"
- ☐ Rap music
- ☐ The <u>Mona Lisa</u> painting
- ☐ The art of finger painting
- ☐ The Statue of Liberty
- ☐ The Golden Gate Bridge
- ☐ Pikes Peak in the Rockies
- ☐ Moon rocks

A B C D E F G H

Invention or Discovery?

Students distinguish discoveries (finding something that already exists) from inventions (creating something new).

Background

Species of plants and animals are being discovered every day. They're being invented, too. Gene-splicing and selective breeding are creating whole new organisms for which scientists can win patents. The line between discovery and invention may have become thinner, but it's still solid: Discoveries already exist; discoverers simply find them for the first time. Inventions don't exist until someone creates them.

> **"Build a better mousetrap, and the world will beat a path to your door."**
> —*Ralph Waldo Emerson*

RESEARCH: How does this statement apply to a modern invention?

Lesson Ideas

Review the items on the "I Spy an Invention" list (page 8). Which ones are inventions? Discoveries? How can certain things be both? For example, plants grow naturally in the wild. When humans find them, the plants are discoveries. But when humans breed the plants into new varieties, the plants are inventions. Hand out reproducible page 10 and challenge students to figure out the missing words from each example on the list. Hint: To complete the activity, encourage students to look for clues in the sentences, use the process of elimination, and consider the time periods mentioned.

Answers

1. gravity, self-draining pool cover 2. Hubble Space Telescope, galaxies
3. sealed tomb, mummy 4. gunpowder, guns 5. lightning rod, electricity.
Bonus: See Lesson Ideas, above.

💡 Extension

During a unit on the voyages of explorers, have students keep a log of inventions and discoveries that they encounter. Explorers (both ancient and modern) rely heavily on the latest technology to stay safe and healthy while isolated for a long period of time. Navigation equipment (compass, sextant, satellite tracking), new Arctic-weather fabrics (waterproof polyester, Gortex fabric), and convenience foods (smoked or salted foods, canned and freeze-dried meals) are just a few examples. Discoveries include any natural object that the explorers saw for the first time: a view of the entire Earth from space, for example.

Invention or Discovery?

What's the difference between an invention and a discovery? Read each example. Then write in the missing words from the list.

Word List
electricity
galaxies
gravity
gunpowder
guns
Hubble Space Telescope
lightning rod
mummy
sealed tomb
self-draining pool cover

1. You can use a discovery to create an invention.

Sir Isaac Newton discovered _____.

Teenager Emma Tillman used it to invent a _____.

2. You can use an invention to discover something.

The 1990 invention of the _____ led to the 1996 discovery

of new _____.

3. One discovery can lead to another.

The discovery of a _____ in Egypt led to the discovery

of King Tut's _____.

4. One invention can lead to another.

The invention of _____ in seventh-century China led to

the invention of _____ in medieval Europe.

5. One person can be both an inventor and a discoverer.

Benjamin Franklin's invention of a _____ led to his discovery

of _____.

💡 **BONUS: Humans have both invented tulips and discovered tulips. Explain how.**

Happy Accidents

Students solve clues to complete an acrostic puzzle about accidental inventions.

Background

Inventing by accident doesn't mean sitting back and letting it happen. Just the opposite. It means actively recognizing an invention for what it is and putting it to use. For example, plenty of ancient Arabian travelers probably curdled milk in a pouch made from a sheep's stomach by accident. But not all of them recognized the result as a new food—cheese. Of those who did, few experimented with ways to improve it, package it, and market it.

Lesson Ideas

Pass around an unidentified sample of Silly Putty™ and explain that it is a failed invention. (Or substitute a small bowl of a similar, but slimier, substance by combining cornstarch and water in a ratio of roughly 5 to 3. Add food coloring. Then adjust the ingredients until the substance is half liquid and half solid. After use, *do not* pour it down a drain, as it will clog pipes.)

What do students think of this failure? Is it useless? Should you throw it out? After students recognize the Silly Putty™ or you disclose what it is, encourage them to explore its properties. Why is this "failure" a successful toy? What does it do? If it weren't a toy, what else could it be?

Explain that in 1941 General Electric wanted to create a new artificial rubber to replace imported rubber during World War II. Instead, a GE engineer named James Wright ended up with a stretchy, non-rotting blob made of boric acid and silicone oil. The owner of a toy shop liked how the blob felt and sold it as "nutty putty." Later, with a new name and an egg-shaped case, the Silly Putty™ "failure" hit the top of the toy charts.

Have students do the activity on reproducible page 12 to learn about some of these "happy accidents."

Answers

1. hot tea 2. earl of Sandwich 3. cheese 4. Post-it Note 5. vacuum and rug 6. fungi called mold **Quotation:** "Name the greatest of all inventors. Accident."

💡 Extension

Books such as *811 Mistakes that Worked* by Charlotte Foltz Jones (Doubleday, 1991) feature more examples of accidental inventions: Teflon™, Ivory™ soap, ice cream, flying ring toys, Scotchguard™, and the like. Have students research an accidental invention and write a historical fiction story that describes who was there when it was created, what might have been said, and how people may have reacted to the invention.

> "An invention does not have to be a huge new machine or something that will change the world. An invention may be an old idea with a new twist or improvement."
> —*Lauren Patricia DeLuca (student inventor)*

EXPERIMENT: Think of an object you see every day. What would you do to improve it?

Happy Accidents

Sometimes people invent things by accident. Read each "happy accident" clue below. Fill in as many as you can. Then copy the letters into the puzzle. If you get stuck, work backward. Fill in words in the puzzle. Then transfer the letters back to the clues. The finished puzzle spells out an "inventive" quotation.

1. **China, 2737 B.C.:** Emperor Shen Nung was boiling water outdoors. Leaves fell into the pot. Minutes later, Shen Nung had accidentally invented

   H __ __ __ __ __ .
   27 37 15 24 18

2. **England, 1762:** John Montagu wanted to eat lunch but keep one hand free. So he put meat between two slices of bread. This unplanned invention was named after Montagu, the

   __ __ __ __ OF
   7 30 9 19

   S __ __ __ W __ __ __ .
   2 22 34 21 31 6

3. **Ancient Arabia, date unknown:** A traveler poured milk into a pouch made out of a sheep's stomach. Later, he later opened the pouch to take a drink. But the desert sun and stomach juices had turned the milk into the first

   CH __ __ __ __ .
   35 13 14 10

4. **United States, 1970s:** Spencer Silver tried to invent a super-strong glue. Instead he invented a super-weak one. Silver spread the weak glue on scrap paper to make a

   PO __ __ - __ __ __ O __ __ .
   29 5 33 12 25 26 4

5. **United States, 1990s:** Seventh grader Jennifer Garcia hated cleaning the floor after tracking mud in the house. She found that it was easier to clean her shoes instead. Jennifer invented a mat that's an all-in-one

   __ __ __ UU __
   23 11 32 3

   A N D __ UG.
     1   28

6. **England, 1928:** Alexander Fleming was experimenting with bacteria. Tiny particles landed on his experiment. The bacteria died. Fleming had accidentally found a future medicine—penicillin. The tiny particles were

   __ U __ __ I CALLED M __ __ D.
   17 36 8   16 20

Author Mark Twain said: " N __ __ __ __ __ __
                               1 2 3 4 5 6 7

__ __ __ __ __ __ __ __
8 9 10 11 12 13 14 15

__ __ __ __ __ . __ __ __ __ __ __ __ __ **"**
16 17 18 19 20   30 31 32 33 34 35 36 37

__ __ __ __ __ __ __ __ __
21 22 23 24 25 26 27 28 29

Nature Invents

Students match inventions with the natural structures that inspired them. They then generate invention ideas based on the natural design of a honeycomb.

Background

Think of nature as an inventor, and the whole world takes on new meaning. Teeth become chisels. A tuna looks like a high-speed submarine. Squid act like tiny jet engines, propelling themselves forward by blowing streams of water backward. The twisted tips of buzzard wings are stabilizers—wire-controlled flaps for steering airplanes. The ear is a model for the telephone. The eye is a sophisticated camera.

In a sense, nature is the queen of inventors, creating mechanisms, materials, and designs to cope with every situation on Earth. For this reason, combining a lesson on plant and animal adaptations with a lesson on the science of invention couldn't be more natural.

Lesson Ideas

If you had to invent an animal to survive in a hot, sand-swept desert, what would the creature look like? How would it cope with a lack of water and drastic swings of temperature? What devices would help it move in the sand? What defenses would protect it from dangerous sandstorms? How would it find and eat food? What enemies would it have? Incorporate students' ideas into a sketch. Then display a picture of a camel. What natural inventions do students see in the camel? What tools or defenses does it have for coping with the desert? Examples:

- ◆ Extra-long eyelashes to keep out sand

- ◆ Nostrils that shut tight for the same reason

- ◆ Split hooves that spread out when the camel walks, keeping its legs from sinking in the soft sand

- ◆ Fat in a hump so that the rest of the body can cool off

- ◆ Internal mechanisms for doing without food and water for a long time.

Reproducible page 15 asks students to compare a variety of natural inventions with the actual human-made inventions that nature inspired. Reproducible page 16 is a more open-ended exercise that challenges teams of students to think about natural designs and use critical-thinking skills to draw analogies with human-made inventions. Stress that each natural design can have many similar inventions; there's no single right answer.

> **"Every generation must go further than the last, or what's the use in it?"**
> —*Meridel Le Sueur*

DISCUSS: Will we ever reach the point where we can't improve anymore?

Answers

PAGE 15 1. B 2. A 3. G 4. C 5. D 6. H 7. E 8. F **PAGE 16** Ask teams to explain their answers and accept all reasonable ideas. Sample ideas: **1.** Gothic cathedrals, space shuttles or rockets on the launchpad **2.** track shoes with spikes, grappling hooks, mountain climber's pickax **3.** cement, adobe, dried mud bricks **4.** military camouflage **5.** suits of armor, curving train cars, tanks, accordions **6.** barbed wire **7.** ballast tanks on submarines, inflatable beach toys, rafts **8.** Morse code lamps, searchlights, buoys, lighthouses **9.** helmets, domed sports arenas **10.** solar panels **11.** flypaper, adhesive tapes **12.** waxed fruit, skin lotion

💡 Extensions

Students can discover natural inventions (or adaptations) on every animal or plant. *Nature Got There First* by Phil Gates (Kingfisher, 1995) is an excellent reference for students. *The Private Eye: Looking and Thinking by Analogy* by Kerry Ruef (The Private Eye Project, 1992) is a curriculum based on making observations and analogies about objects, including natural ones. *The Robot Zoo: A Mechanical Guide to the Way Animals Work* by John Kelly (Turner Publishing, 1994) is an extraordinary visual reference that substitutes machines for the body parts of animals—springs for the leg muscles of a grasshopper, for example.

A honeycomb is a network of hexagons (six-sided shapes). Bees use honeycombs to store honey and raise their young. Challenge students to use the design of the honeycomb to create their own invention. Here are a few tips to get them started:

◆ A hexagon is a very strong and sturdy shape for building.

◆ Hexagons fit together perfectly, with no spaces between them.

◆ Each compartment is the same size and shape.

◆ Queen bees lay one egg per compartment.

◆ To make the honeycomb bigger, bees just add more hexagons. This type of design is called modular.

Students may want to investigate and modify existing honeycomblike inventions. For example, quilters, floor tilers, designers, and architects (among others) use hexagons to create repeating patterns. An egg carton has one egg per compartment. So do many shipping crates packed with fruit. Space labs and space stations have a modular design so that they can expand or shrink piece by piece in space.

Nature Invents: Match-Up

In 1948, Swiss engineer George de Mestral (duh-miss-TRAL) went for a walk in a field. Burrs (spiky plant seeds) clung to his clothing. De Mestral studied the burrs. He found that they had hundreds of tiny hooks. No wonder they clung so tightly! De Mestral copied the tiny hooks. Then he made a fabric with tiny loops for the hooks to grab. His invention is now called Velcro™.

Nature gives inventors endless ideas. The trick is to put them to good use, as de Mestral did. Match the natural facts with the human inventions below.

Natural Facts

_____ 1. Zebra mussels cling hard and fast to rocks, pipes, and ships.

_____ 2. For its weight, spider silk is stronger than steel.

_____ 3. Cats' eyes glow in the dark.

_____ 4. Whales navigate by echolocation: making sounds and listening for the echoes.

_____ 5. Foods spoil and bodies decay (rot) more slowly in the desert.

_____ 6. Caribou hooves split and spread out each time they step. This keeps the animal from sinking in soft mud or snow.

_____ 7. Dolphins have long, round, tapered bodies in the shape of cigars.

_____ 8. Maple leaf seeds rotate as they glide to the ground.

Human Inventions

A. Bulletproof vests

B. One of the world's strongest glues

C. Sonar for mapping the ocean floor

D. Mummies

E. Silent and swift submarines

F. Helicopters

G. Road reflectors for safer driving

H. Snowshoes

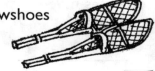

Nature Invents: Your Turn

Here's a list of natural inventions. For each one, name a similar human invention. There are many possible answers. Be ready to explain yours.

1. Many rain forest trees have above-ground supports called buttresses or stilts.

_____

2. Claws help bears, cats, and dogs to grip soft surfaces while they run.

_____

3. Termites mix saliva, dirt, and dung to make rock-hard mounds.

_____

4. A jaguar's spots blend in with the light and dark shadows in a forest.

_____

5. Armadillos have hard plates of bone. Gaps between the plates allow the armadillo to roll into a ball.

_____

6. Roses have sharp thorns to keep attackers away.

_____

7. Swim bladders that inflate and deflate help fish rise and sink in water.

_____

8. Fireflies use a flashing light to signal their mates.

_____

9. The *Pachycephalosaurus* (pak-ee-SEFF-uh-luh-SAWR-us) dinosaur had a hard, domed-shaped head.

_____

10. Reptiles bask in the sun to collect heat energy.

_____

11. The sundew plant has sticky hairlike threads to trap flies.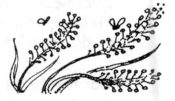

_____

12. Many desert plants have a wax coating on their leaves to keep in moisture.

_____

Bicycle Built for Technology

Students compare an early bicycle with a modern one to discover how inventions are made of many smaller inventions and how and why bicycle design changed.

Curriculum Connections
✓ Science
✓ Math
✓ Critical-Thinking Skills

Background

Every modern invention depends on many inventions before it. Cell phones appeared only after satellites went into orbit. Antibiotics and vaccines followed the microscope. The internal combustion engine made motor vehicles possible. Like these inventions, the modern bicycle appeared after all the necessary technology fell into place—steel, pneumatic (inflated) tires, ball bearings, and so on.

Primitive bicycle models of the early 1800s had no pedals; people pushed along with their feet on the ground. Many of the first pedaled bicycles in the 1870s had extremely large front wheels and tiny back wheels, no gears or chains, pedals attached to the center of the front wheel, and a dizzying six-foot-high seat. Why such a high seat? The rider had to pedal exactly as fast as the front wheel turned. The high seat brought the rider's pedaling legs in line with the pedals and the wheel. The introduction of gears and chains controlled the rate of pedaling, and so bicycle wheels shrank and became equal in size. The rider sat in between the wheels at a reasonable height instead of high on top of the front wheel.

The velocipede ("foot speed"), as the early bicycle was called, went through rapid design changes thanks to advances in materials and machine parts. Inventors filed hundreds of patents. There were 30 patents alone for a split-skirt outfit that allowed Victorian women to maintain modesty while riding! Though we still ride a two-wheeler with a saddle and handlebars, the modern bicycle now comes in a wide array of models. The specialized designs make the bicycles more efficient at certain functions. Examples:

◆ Long-distance bikes have large, thin tires (to achieve more distance per pedal and give a smoother ride), comfortable saddles and handlebars, and several gears for going up and down hills.

◆ Racing bikes such as the state-of-the-art 1996 U.S. Olympic bicycle are very lightweight and aerodynamic with minimal handlebars, no brakes, and a solid rear wheel (to reduce air turbulence).

◆ Rough terrain or mountain bikes have smaller and fatter wheels (to withstand bumps), shorter handlebars (for better control), and a heavier, sturdier frame.

◆ Load-bearing bikes have special attachments for carrying objects, fat tires, and a sturdy frame.

◆ General purpose bikes have medium wheels and tires and a sturdy but not rugged frame.

Lesson Ideas

Reproducible page 19 shows the parts of an old-fashioned bicycle. Which parts still exist? Which ones don't? Which ones have changed—and how? Students will be able to answer these questions by comparing the diagram to their own bicycle at home or at school, or a picture of a modern bicycle. Reproducible page 20 asks students to compare bicycle designs by measuring the features of different bicycles.

Scour old biking magazines for examples of various bicycle designs and have students classify them by purpose: general use, long-distance travel, racing, rough terrain, and heavy cargo. What features do the bicycles in each group have in common? How might these features make the bicycle better at its job? For example, what types of bikes have big wheels? How does a big wheel help a long-distance rider? *(cushier ride; more distance per pedal)*

◆ How does a small wheel help a mountain biker? *(easier to turn; lower to the ground for more stability)*

◆ Why are the handlebars different? Hint: Which bikes have to be comfortable and which ones have to be easy to control?

◆ Are the spokes spread out or close together? How does this affect the flow of air? *(An open-spoked wheel lets air through more easily and so is easier to turn left or right.)*

◆ What is the trail size? (See Reproducible page 20.) Which type of bikes need to be more stable? Which ones need to be easy to turn?

Answers

PAGE 19 1. possibly all except for pedals on the front wheel and a smaller rear wheel 2. Accept reasonable answers. 3. chain, gears, modern handlebars, water bottle, and so on **PAGE 20** Answers will vary, depending on the model of bicycle. In general, bike shops size models by the wheel diameter (26 inches, for example) and classify them by use. Bicycles built for stability, such as children's bicycles, have a larger trail size.

💡 Extension

Have students identify, investigate, and make a drawing that shows the many small inventions inside a big invention of their choice, such as in-line skates, skateboards, pencil sharpeners, or even the automobile. They can use "how it works" references such as books by David Macaulay and Stephen Biesty to label the parts. Some smaller inventions date to ancient or prehistoric times: the wheel, gears, steel, and iron, for example. Others, such as the chain (1897) and multiple gears (1889), are more recent.

Bicycle Built for Technology, Part 1

Bicycles are many inventions rolled into one.
Here are some of the parts in a bicycle built in the 1880s.

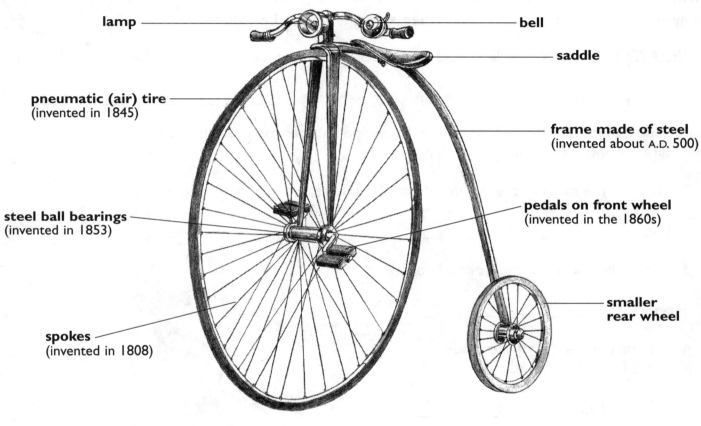

lamp — bell

saddle

pneumatic (air) tire
(invented in 1845)

frame made of steel
(invented about A.D. 500)

steel ball bearings
(invented in 1853)

pedals on front wheel
(invented in the 1860s)

smaller
rear wheel

spokes
(invented in 1808)

1. Which parts can you find on a modern bike? _____

_____

_____

2. How have the parts changed? _____

_____

_____

3. What modern parts does this bike lack? _____

_____

_____

Bicycle Built for Technology, Part 2

Why do bicycles have different designs? Measure the features of a bicycle. Then compare your measurements to those of other teams.

What You Need: bicycle ◆ measuring stick ◆ masking tape

Bicycle Type (distance, speed, mountain, cargo, general): _____

1. Tape a mark on the bike's front tire. Then tape another mark on the floor directly under the axle (see drawing).

2. Measure the radius—the distance from the axle to the outside of the tire.

   Radius: _____

3. Count the spokes in the front wheel.

   Spokes: _____

4. Measure the height of the saddle (seat) from the ground.

   Saddle height: _____

5. Use the back of this page to draw and describe the handlebars.

6. The trail size tells how stable (steady) a bicycle is. The bigger the trail size, the steadier the bike. Place a stick along the fork from the handlebars to the floor. Mark where the stick touches the floor. Measure the distance between this mark and the floor mark under the axle.

   Trail size: _____

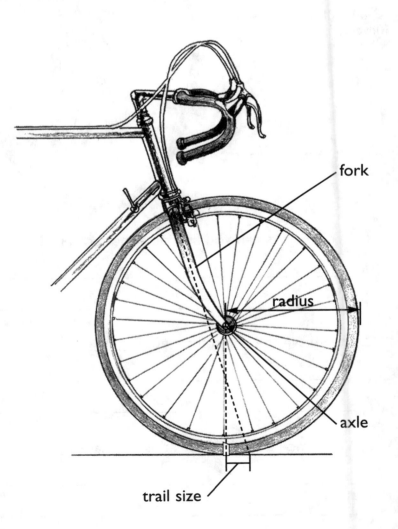

(Science) Fiction or Fact?

Students use logic and basic science knowledge to classify inventions into three categories: those that exist already, those that don't exist but are possible, and those that are pure science fiction.

Background

Science fiction is the genre of literature that uses scientific ideas to create fictional stories. Sometimes, science fiction writers invent fantastical devices that later become reality. For example, in Jules Verne's *20,000 Leagues Under the Sea* (1870), Captain Nemo explores the ocean bottom in a high-tech submarine with electric lights and Aqua-Lung-type devices on board. Electric lights were invented shortly after publication, Aqua-Lungs™ appeared in 1943, and high-tech submarines arrived in the 1950s.

Here are more examples of visionary science fiction:

◆ In 1626, Sir Francis Bacon predicted lasers, a twentieth-century invention.

◆ In 1657, Cyrano de Bergerac was among the first of many writers to tell a tale of rockets to the moon, a late 1960s event.

◆ In the 1940s, Arthur C. Clarke wrote about human-made objects that orbited Earth. Satellites were invented in 1959.

◆ H. G. Wells "invented" air bombs and atomic bombs well before their time.

◆ Isaac Asimov envisioned the pocket calculator in 1950; it became a reality in the 1990s.

Of course, many science fiction devices stayed and will most probably stay in the realm of make-believe. These "inventions" defy the laws of science:

◆ De Bergerac's other methods for getting to the moon, including floating on the power of evaporating water.

◆ Time machines, such as the one H. G. Wells imagined in the late 19th century to transport people forward and backward in time and the one featured in the *Back to the Future* movie trilogy of the 1980s.

◆ *Star Trek*'s "warp" speed or any other speed that's faster than light.

◆ Travel between stars and galaxies.

◆ Any type of sound in space, which is a vacuum and therefore can't carry sounds.

For more information, check resources such as *The Science in Science Fiction* by Peter Nicholls (Knopf, 1983), *Science Fiction, Science Fact* by Isaac Asimov (Gareth Stevens, 1989), and *The Physics of Star Trek* (HarperCollins,1996).

Lesson Ideas

Hand out reproducible page 23. Students may not have all the science knowledge required to sort fact from fiction in this activity, but they can use common sense and make educated guesses. Point out that even the predictions of experts often turn out wrong (many said moon travel was impossible, for example). The idea is for students to apply what they do know—Newton's laws of motion, how sound travels, the speed of light—to the gadgets and gizmos they see on TV and in the movies.

Answers

1. Fiction **2.** Fiction (It would take hundreds or thousands of years.) **3.** Future Fact (*2001: A Space Odyssey* explored the idea of centripetal force—a spinning spaceship—to simulate the force of gravity. *Star Trek VI* made use of magnetic "gravity boots.") **4.** Fiction (There is no sound in space.) **5.** Fiction (You can't feel light as a solid object.) **6.** Fact (Once perfected, all computers may soon use voice commands.) **7.** Fiction **8.** Fact (Lasers are used routinely to burn away tumors or human tissue during surgery. Laser weapons are part of the U.S. military's arsenal.) **9.** Fact or Future Fact (Russian cosmonauts orbit Earth for months.) **10.** Future Fact (Engineers are developing insectlike robots for that very purpose.)

Extensions

Current science fiction books, television shows, and movies are churning out new ideas for the future. Have students make a list of the futuristic gadgets or concepts in a short story, TV show, or movie. Which ones do they think have the best chance of becoming reality?

Choose half a dozen clever and interesting devices from science fiction stories and challenge students to write a patent request, including a drawing and a "how it works" explanation. (For more on patents, see "Parts of a Patent," page 92.)

> *"Technology makes more technology possible."*
> —*Alvin Toffler*

DEBATE: Do you think technology will destroy humanity or save it?

(Science) Fiction or Fact?

Fiction is make-believe. Fact is real. Science fiction writers combine both fiction and fact to create stories. Can you tell the difference?

Read about the inventions below. If you think an invention exists now, check the box under "Fact." If you think the invention could exist in the future, check "Future Fact." The "Fiction" column is for inventions that you believe are and will be impossible.

Invention	Fact	Future Fact	Fiction
1. Spaceships traveling faster than light			
2. Humans traveling to other star systems			
3. Artificial (fake) gravity so that astronauts feel as if they're on Earth			
4. Starships that make a deafening noise in space			
5. 3-D holograms (light images) that look and feel real			
6. Computers that respond to human voice commands			
7. Transporters that make a person disappear and then reappear far away			
8. Light rays that can kill			
9. People living on a space station			
10. Robot miners working on the moon			

Debate: Who Owns the Cure?

Working in groups of five, students each take a role and a position in a debate about a new but overpriced cure for cancer. Their goal is to decide who—if anyone—should own a patent for the medicine.

Background

Inventions belong to the inventor. But is there ever a time when other concerns overrule an inventor's right to his or her creation? Unprecedented advances in medicine during the 1980s and 1990s have produced a boom market for life-and-death drugs, especially for diseases like cancer. The spread of cancer, AIDS, and other diseases has created a growing population of patients who need these rare and expensive drugs but can't afford them. The annual tab per person can reach well into the tens of thousands of dollars.

Lesson Ideas

The debate on reproducible page 25 is geared toward sixth, seventh, and eighth graders. Use your discretion as to whether this activity is appropriate to do with your students as the questions raised are are delicate and complex and have no easy answers: Do all terminal patients have the right to treatment? Who should pay for this treatment? Should a drug company monopolize this type of market because it owns a patent? Should it make a profit on life-and-death drugs? And if it doesn't make a profit, who will pay for research and development?

Newspaper clippings of actual medical cases will help lay the groundwork. After dividing the class into groups and assigning roles (see page 26), have all students in the same role meet and discuss their position. For example, all the patients should get together and brainstorm a list of arguments and then return to their debate groups.

💡 Extension

Another rich discussion topic is the concept that plants and animals can now be patented inventions. Scientists create new organisms by splicing together genes of different organisms, by breeding for certain traits, or by cloning genetic duplicates of existing organisms. Hybrid plants and lines of laboratory cells (such as cells susceptible to cancer) are common examples. Scientists are also now beginning to patent breeds for more advanced animals.

Who Owns the Cure?

Cutting Edge Chemicals has invented a cure for cancer called Getawell. The company has a patent, meaning other companies can't copy the cure. In order to profit, Cutting Edge charges a very high price. Some patients can't afford it. Your group has been asked to seek a solution that's fair to everyone. Your goal is to agree on answers to the questions below, then be ready to explain your position.

1. Should Cutting Edge keep its patent? Why or why not? _____

_____

_____

_____

2. Should Cutting Edge share or give up its patent? If so, who will pay for the company's research

debt? _____

_____

_____

_____

3. Should the government pass a law banning patents for medicines for terminal diseases?

Why or why not? _____

_____

_____

_____

4. Who—if anyone—should pay for patients to have medicine? How should the cost be divided?

_____

_____

_____

_____

President, Cutting Edge Chemicals

You are in business to make money. Otherwise, your employees lose jobs and Cutting Edge can't make medicine. Getawell cost millions of dollars to invent. The patent helps you earn back your money before having to compete with other companies. You'll fight hard to keep your patent and to keep making money.

Cancer Patient

Getawell costs $10,000 per year! You want the government to take back the patent on this medicine. That way, companies will compete to make Getawell and the price will go down. The real cost of Getawell is one-tenth the price that Cutting Edge is charging. And even if it weren't, the government—or someone—should make up the difference. This is life or death!

Cancer Doctor

Naturally, you side with your patients. You believe that everyone, rich or poor, has the right to treatment. But you don't think the government should foot the whole bill. Neither should Cutting Edge or the insurance companies. The burden is just too great. Perhaps there's a new approach to solving this problem—a middle ground for everyone to stand on.

U.S. Senator

You introduce bills that might become laws. Most citizens in your state believe that medicines for terminal diseases should be patent-free. That means any company can make and sell the medicines. On the other hand, Cutting Edge has donated a lot of money to your campaign.

President, High-Tech, Inc.

You'd love to see the patent on Getawell dropped. Your company could then make and sell the medicine. You might even be able to do it more cheaply than Cutting Edge. But what about your own inventions? If Cutting Edge can't protect its life-or-death medicines, then you won't be able to protect yours.

Inventions Past, Present, and Future

From 1878 to 1888, many Americans were petrified of fire. The great Chicago fire and other frightful blazes had given people good cause for alarm. In one year alone, inventors filed dozens of patents for new fire safety devices: bridges, chutes, ladders, cages, alarms, and more.

Throughout history, events have spawned inventions, and inventions have influenced events. Entire time periods—the Bronze Age, the Industrial Revolution, the Space Age—are named for history-altering inventions.

In this section, students research and write trading cards about inventors, choose the world's ten greatest inventions, interview senior citizens, compare clocks and transportation methods of the past, imagine new uses for old tools, write a "historical" speech for a new invention, distinguish true inventions from fraudulent ones, and predict automobile designs of the future.

Inventor Trading Cards

Students research the life of an inventor to write biographical trading cards.

Curriculum Connections
✓ Social Studies
✓ Language Arts

Mark Twain

Background

Inventors come from every corner of the world and every point in human history. They are young and old, male and female, rich and poor. Not all of them are scientists or engineers. American author Mark Twain received several patents, one for a new design of suspenders. President Abraham Lincoln received a patent for his invention of a navigation tool. A seamstress known only as "Mrs. Samuel Slater" on her patent application invented cotton sewing thread in 1773. She was the first American woman to receive a patent.

Lesson Ideas

Reproducible page 30 provides a model for students to follow as they research and write their own trading cards. Make multiple copies of the bottom half of the page for students to use. Reproducible page 31 includes a list of inventors who make interesting subjects. Students will have no trouble finding information on well-known inventors—Thomas Edison, Leonardo da Vinci, Eli Whitney, and the like. Biographies of lesser-known inventors tend to be lumped into general books about "women inventors" or "African-American inventors." Both types of books are listed in Resources (see page 95). If students have difficulty locating photos or pictures of any of the inventors, they can draw a picture of the inventor's invention.

Another approach to researching inventors might yield a greater variety of subjects. Students can choose a favorite field (clothing, transportation, music, etc.) and research the inventions in that field. In the process, they will learn new names and faces to put on a trading card.

A third approach is for students to report on all the inventors who contributed to one large invention such as the automobile, the airplane, or the computer. For example, thinkers such as Roger Bacon were envisioning self-propelled vehicles from the 13th century on. Leonardo da Vinci and others designed machines for flying; the Wright Brothers happened to make their design work and so got all the glory. The computer started with the ancient Chinese abacus and included a series of calculating machines in the 16th to 20th centuries.

> **"I invent nothing. I rediscover."**
> —*Auguste Rodin*

RESEARCH: Find an old invention that is no longer used. How could you reinvent it to bring it up to date?

💡 Extension

Students can use their trading cards to play "Name That Inventor." Two players split the deck in half. Each player draws the top card of his or her deck and covers the name of the inventor with a finger so that the opponent can see only the picture.

Player 1 reads the top clue (nationality) on his or her card and says, "Name that inventor!" If Player 2 can name the inventor, he or she wins Player 1's card and places it in a "win" pile. Then Player 1 draws a new card and Player 2 gets another chance to name the inventor and win a card, as above.

If Player 2 can't name the inventor, Player 1 holds onto the card and Player 2 reads the top clue on his or her own card. If Player 1 names the inventor, he or she wins *both* cards. Both players then draw new cards and play another round, switching the order of play (Player 2 reads a clue first).

If both players miss the first clue, they move on to the second clue (year born) and then the third clue (major inventions). If no one guesses correctly, players set aside the cards and draw two new ones. The game ends after all cards have been played. The winner is the player with more cards.

When students first play the game, they may have little success at naming lesser-known inventors. But through repeated play, students will learn to recognize and identify them.

Inventor: _Lady Ada Lovelace_

> *"When I was a girl I wished that I had been a boy because a boy could find work to make money, and there was nothing a girl could do to earn money. I feel now that . . . I am glad I was a girl."*
>
> —*Cathy Evans*

DISCUSS: Evans invented a popular way to make bedspreads. Her business put food on the table but never made her rich. How might Evans's life have been different if she had lived in the 1980s instead of the 1880s? How have attitudes toward women in business changed? Can a small, home-based industry succeed today?

The Patriotic Inventor

Beulah Louise Henry held 52 patents. But she never became as famous as her Revolutionary ancestor, Patrick Henry. In the 1920s and 1930s, she invented a hair curler, an umbrella, a sewing machine, a "Miss Illusion" doll (its blue eyes changed to brown and brown hair changed to blonde), and much more. Henry had a rare condition called synethesia. It caused her to perceive sound as color and taste as touch. The condition may also explain how Henry made complex drawings without mechanical training or scientific knowledge.

Inventor Trading Cards

Research an inventor. Then fill out a trading card. Paste or draw a picture of the inventor in the frame. Cut out and color the card. Fold it in half (blank part inside) and tape or paste it shut.

Nationality: Great Britain

Year Born: 1815

Major Inventions: Computer programming language

Mini-Bio: A whiz at math, Lady Ada Lovelace hooked up with scientist Charles Babbage. Babbage invented the forerunner of the computer. Lovelace invented a program to run the machine. Her program was a series of cards with holes. The pattern of holes told the machine how to calculate. Neither Lovelace nor Babbage got rich. In fact, Lovelace lost a fortune and died of cancer at age 36.

Inventor: Lady Ada Lovelace

Nationality: _____

Year Born: _____

Major Inventions: _____

_____

Mini-Bio: _____

_____

_____

_____

_____

_____

_____

_____

Inventor: _____

Inventors, Famous and Not-So-Famous

Elizabeth Arden
cosmetics

Alexander Graham Bell
telephone

Mary Carpenter
factory machines

Marie Curie
radiation counter

John Deere
farm machines

Thomas Edison
phonograph, lightbulb

Harold Edgerton
strobe light

Gertrude Elion
medicines

Enrico Fermi
atomic reactor

Benjamin Franklin
bifocals, rocking chair

Clara Frye
bed for the infirm

Robert Goddard
liquid fuel rocket

Charles Goodyear
rubber

Johannes Gutenberg
printing press

Ruth Handler
Barbie doll

Beulah Louise Henry
sewing machine

Admiral Grace Hopper
computer programming

Thiphena Hornbrook
apiary or beehive

Elias Howe
sewing machine

Hypatia
astrolabe, hydroscope

Harriet Irwin
hexagon-shaped house

Beatrice Kenner
self-oiling hinge

Mary Kies
braided straw bonnets

Margaret Knight
brown paper grocery bag

Stephanie Louise Kwolek
Kevlar™, a stronger-than-steel material

Hedy Lamarr
secret wartime communications system

Gugliemo Marconi
radio

John Matzeliger
shoe-making machine

Elijah McCoy
automatic oil cup to keep trains running smoothly

Elizabeth Miller
women's bloomers

Mildred Mitchell
bionics—electronic copies of living things

Samuel Morse
telegraph, Morse code

Hannah Mountain
life-preserving mattress for boats

James Naismith
basketball

Francis and Gertrude Rogallo
batwinged kite, now called a hang glider

Ralph Samuelson
water skis

Francis and Freeland Stanley
Stanley Steamer automobile

Nikola Tesla
electromagnetic motor

Harriet Tracy
safety elevator to slow the fall in case of a power failure

Eli Whitney and Catherine Greene
cotton gin

Ruth Wakefield
Toll House™ chocolate chip cookies

George Westinghouse
steam engine, air brake

The World's Ten Greatest Inventions

Teams of students work cooperatively to choose the ten greatest inventions from a list of likely candidates. They then compile the lists into a graph.

Background

Some inventions are so earth-shaking that they merit their own age: the Bronze Age, the Machine Age, the Golden Age of the Automobile, the Space Age, the Computer Age. Other inventions are important because they are ubiquitous: television, clothing, paper, electrical power. Still other inventions have the distinction of antiquity: the wheel, pottery, bricks, the alphabet, and so on.

Many people have arranged inventions into top 10, top 50, or even top 100 lists. And every list is different. No matter. It's the process, not the result, that counts. This mental exercise prompts students to use logic, reasoning, and knowledge to examine priorities—their own and society's.

Lesson Ideas

What makes an invention great? Either provide groups with a single criterion (to make the exercise easier and more concrete) or generate a list of criteria through discussion, such as:

✓ Makes people's lives easier

✓ Brings happiness

✓ Saves lives

✓ Saves people from boring or hard work

✓ Advances science or technology

✓ Has been used for a long time or by a lot of people

Are all of these criteria equally important? Or do some matter more? Split the class into teams of three or four students and give the teams a few minutes to discuss or decide on criteria for a great invention. Then distribute reproducible page 34. Each team has 15 to 20 minutes to agree on a list of ten all-time top inventions.

Compare lists and discuss some of the issues that arose. Why did groups include or omit certain inventions? Are new inventions (printing press, typewriter, computer) greater than old inventions (paper, ink) or vice versa? Old inventions were more directly connected with basic human survival: better farming, housing, and clothing, for example. But new inventions may affect more people at a faster rate, thanks to our greater global connectedness.

Can "bad" or destructive inventions (nuclear power, gunpowder) ever be great? Chinese societies who invented gunpowder didn't use it as a weapon. Their powder kegs were used for entertaining fireworks. Nuclear power created weapons. But it's also a renewable form of energy that could reduce our dependence on polluting, nonrenewable energy such as fossil fuels.

Is it more important to know where you are (compass, map) or what time it is (clock, sundial)? Are diversions (baseball, movies) ever as important as useful inventions (refrigerator, microwave)? If not, why do we pay our entertainers so much more than our scientists, inventors, and engineers?

Have students interpret and graph the data. A simple bar graph can show which inventions were mentioned most often. A more complex graph can weigh the inventions by their ratings. Here's one method:

◆ Convert the rankings into a point system (a "1" ranking earns 10 points, a "2" ranking earns 9 points, and so on).

◆ Total the points for each invention on each list.

◆ Divide the totals by the number of times each invention appeared on a list.

◆ Graph the inventions by their average scores.

> "It was an unfortunate accident that this discovery [nuclear fission] came about in time of war. I have not worked on smashing the atom with the idea of producing death-dealing weapons."
> —*Lise Meitner*

RESEARCH: Nuclear fission made atomic weapons and nuclear power plants possible. What other war inventions had peacetime uses?

💡 Extensions

Publish your results in a school newsletter or send them to a local newspaper in the form of a press release. Include a short blurb about each invention.

Ask students to imagine life without one of the great inventions. Who would suffer most? Would anyone benefit? Can something else take its place? Have them choose an invention from the class compilation and write a diary entry of a typical family on a day without the invention.

Invention Poll

If you were marooned on an island and could have only one invention, what would it be? Have students take a poll and graph the results.

A 1996 survey in *Business Week* magazine asked Americans to name inventions that they couldn't live without.

Invention	Percent
Car	63%
Lightbulb	54%
Telephone	42%
Television	22%
Aspirin	19%
Microwave	13%
Blow-dryer	7.8%
Computer	7.6%

The World's Ten Greatest Inventions

Which inventions are the greatest of all time? Why? Write in your ten choices below. Be ready to explain why you included or left out certain inventions.

airplane
alphabet
automobile
baseball
brick
clock
compass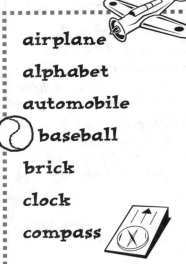

computer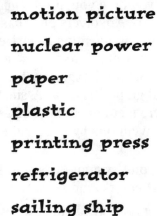
gunpowder
map
matches
microwave
oven
money

motion picture
nuclear power
paper
plastic
printing press
refrigerator
sailing ship

space shuttle
sundial
surgery
telephone
television
other:

_____

1. _____

2. _____

3. _____

4. _____

5. _____

6. _____

7. _____

8. _____

9. _____

10. _____

Where Would We Be?

Students write about the effects of an invention on history.

Curriculum
Connections
✓ Social Studies
✓ Language Arts

Background

Each major invention changes society. Bloomers are no longer around, yet they caused deep changes in the way people viewed women. At the risk of drawing disapproval from scandalized society, women began to wear clothes that were more comfortable and less restricting. They played sports harder. Bloomers can even take partial credit for fueling the women's rights movement.

Or consider churning butter. In the late 19th century, churning butter was one of the most laborious farm chores. No wonder there were almost 2,500 patents for new, improved butter churns! Along with other efficient inventions, the butter churners gave farmworkers—mostly women—more free time. In the 1860s and 1870s, the patent office experienced a boom in patents for farm machinery. Many patents were from women who ran the farms solo while their husbands fought in the Civil War. Today, butter churning is a quaint craft of historical interest only. A new butter churn would have almost no effect on our daily lives.

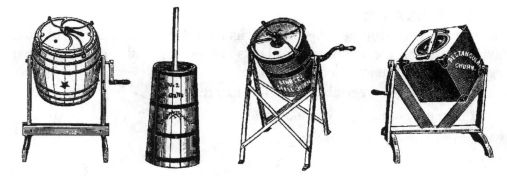

A selection of late nineteenth-century butter churns

Other changes are more complex and more sweeping. Because farm equipment became more efficient in the 19th century, fewer family members were needed at home. Cities swelled with ex-farmers looking for work. The turn-of-the-century invention of cars resulted in a reverse mass movement—families fleeing the cities to live in suburbs.

Telephones brought instant access to anyone in the country. Office innovations increased productivity and shortened the work week. By 1960, television made a politician's physical appearance more important than ever in an election.

Lesson Ideas

Begin by asking students to look at links in their own lives. How do recent inventions such as computers, irradiated foods (they stay fresh longer), skateboards, in-line skates, movie special effects, and the Internet affect them? If humans go to Mars, how might this event change their lives?

Reproducible page 37 can help students explore links between historical events and inventions, but tell them to keep in mind that these links are often subjective and multifaceted. Also, there are more than two possible timelines for every "what if?" question in history. For example, even if bloomers hadn't been invented, freeing women to be more active, other inventions or events might have led to modern women's sports.

Discuss students' responses. Without bloomers, what might women be wearing today? Would clothes be more modest? What types of activities would women be doing?

What would a modern knight look like if knights had continued to be important in battles? (Today's knights carry the title of "sir" and are largely ceremonial.)

How have cowboys changed in the last 100 years? What new inventions do they use to round up cattle or horses? For example, many cowboys have abandoned horses in favor of pick-up trucks.

> "The civilized man has built a coach, but has lost the use of his feet. He is supported on crutches, but lacks so much support of muscle. He has a fine Geneva watch, but he fails of the skill to tell the hour by the sun."
> —*Ralph Waldo Emerson*

DEBATE: Has technology set us back or brought us forward?

💡 Extension

Make a "Wheel of Fortune"–type spinner using a circle and an arrow cut from oaktag. Assemble the spinner with a brass fastener, then label it with a dozen or so "inventive" choices along these lines:

◆ You learn to make vegetables taste like ice cream.

◆ You invent a cure for the common cold.

◆ You invent a way for people to grow taller.

◆ All computers disappear from Earth.

Title the spinner "How would your future life change if . . ." Have each student spin to find out his or her fortune and then write a story about the future. In the story, students should explain how the change of fortune affects them and other people in their lives.

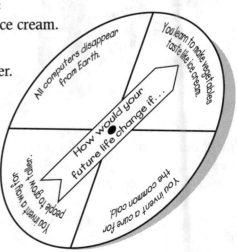

Where Would We Be?

How do inventions change history? Read about the two inventions below. Then choose one and answer the questions in a paragraph on the back.

A. Bloomers (1851)

In the 19th century, women wore long, heavy dresses. The dresses got in the way of sports, gardening, and riding a bicycle.

Elizabeth Miller invented a half-skirt and half-pant outfit. Her "bloomers" freed women to be more active. By the end of the century, women ran, jumped, and sweated in sports such as basketball, baseball, and tennis.

1. Did bloomers lead to modern women's sports? Without them, would women be boxing and playing hockey and football today? Why or why not?

2. What other inventions or events led to women's sports?

B. Cannons and Guns (14th century)

In the Middle Ages, knights had a code of honor called chivalry. These brave warriors fought noble battles on horseback. They wore heavy suits of armor to stop arrows, swords, and other metal weapons.

When soldiers began using guns and cannons, armor became useless. Knights were no longer the most important fighting force. They traded their battle armor for show armor—fancy, colorful costumes. And they traded real battles for jousts—contests to entertain the king.

1. Did guns and cannons end the Age of Chivalry? If these had not been invented, would medieval knights still be around today? Why or why not?

2. What other inventions or events made knights less important as warriors?

A Lifetime Ago

Students interview senior citizens about life without modern inventions.

Background

No one alive today knows firsthand what life was like before bicycles (1870). Only the very oldest humans remember a time without subways (1890), X-rays (1895), and radios (1901). A handful of people can reminisce about the days before household refrigerators (1918) and pop-up toasters (1927), but most senior citizens remember a time before atomic bombs and television (1940s). Middle-aged baby boomers grew up without personal computers, space shuttles, and automatic teller machines (1970s and 1980s). Young adults were born before cellular phones and DNA fingerprinting (1980s and 1990s).

Today's youth, of course, were born into a world with all of these things and more. Just as television shaped the young minds of baby boomers, the Internet and video games are the pop culture of children today.

Lesson Ideas

Students can use reproducible page 39 to make a timeline of inventions for the 20th century. Mark time periods for students (10 years ago), their parents (30 to 40 years ago), their grandparents (50 to 70 years ago), and their great-grandparents (70 to 90 years ago).

How far back can students remember? Their parents? Their grandparents? What inventions were the most important or were changing fast during each lifetime? A few examples: students' great-grandparents witnessed the incredible growth of the automobile and highway systems, their grandparents saw airports spring up in many cities, and their parents witnessed the Space Age take off. We are living in the Age of Information (or Computers).

Using reproducible page 39 for guidance, have students prepare to interview a senior citizen about the decade when the elderly person was 10 years old. Students should complete the personal timeline on the worksheet and research past inventions. A day or so before the interview, they might want to provide interview subjects with old photos and a copy of the reproducible to jog memories. Students can videotape or audiotape the interviews, or just take notes and write a feature story.

💡 Extension

Inventions of the future will make today's "modern" lifestyles seem old-fashioned. Have students work in cooperative groups and imagine that they are 90 years old and are thinking way back to what life was like in the 1990s. Their challenge is to prepare a report, video, visual aid, or other presentation that gives a capsule look at modern life. What is most important to show or tell those not yet born about today's lifestyle? What types of inventions seem most likely to change?

1901

1918

1927

1940

1970

1980

Name _____

A Lifetime Ago

No one alive today remembers the world's first skyscraper being built. It happened in 1882—more than 115 years ago. What *do* senior citizens remember? Interview somebody over 65 years old to find out!

Name of Subject: _____   Age : _____   Year of Birth: _____

1890 1900 1910 1920 1930 1940 1950 1960 1970 1980 1990 2000

1. Mark and label the subject's year of birth on the timeline.

2. Mark and label the decade in which the subject was 10 years old.

3. Mark and label the current year.

4. Research and list at least six inventions that were invented during the decade in which the subject was 10 years old. Gather photos if possible.

5. List interview questions. The questions should help your subject remember daily life when he or she was a child. The questions here will give you some ideas.

Questions

◆ What's the biggest difference between living now and living then?
◆ What hasn't changed at all?
◆ How did you get to school?
◆ What did your hometown look like?
◆ How has it changed?
◆ What toys did you play with?
◆ What did you do after school?
◆ What kind of clothes did you wear?
◆ What modern invention do you wish you had then? Why?

No Time Like the Past

Curriculum Connections
✓ Social Studies
✓ Science
✓ Math

Students research how inventions helped humans measure time in smaller increments. They then experiment with a water clock.

Background

The movements of Earth, the moon, and the sun mark days, months, and years. But ancient humans invented the hour, the minute, and the second. They are arbitrary base-60 measures—units or multiples of 60.

Humans invented accurate methods of measuring time when the need arose. Ancient farmers had to know only seasons—planting time and harvest time. Their day had only two "hours": sunup and sundown. Later, people needed a way to keep track of important events, such as religious festivals. So early astronomers began plotting the days based on moon phases (which gave rise to the lunar calendar) or the sun's movements (which gave rise to the 365-day solar calendar).

Navigation at sea required even more precise measures—hours and minutes. As the great Age of Exploration took off in the 15th to 17th centuries, so did the invention of mechanical and pendulum clocks. The 18th century brought a greater interest in science. Also, the Industrial Revolution put time at a premium as machines had to "work like clockwork" down to the second. By the early 20th century, electronic clocks measured tenths and hundredths of a second. Today's computerized clocks can track thousandths of a second or less.

Lesson Ideas

Ask students to close their eyes. When you say, "Go," they should estimate five seconds of time and then raise their hand and open their eyes. How far off were they? If they didn't have a clock, how would they measure the passage of

a second? A minute? An hour or a day? Why do we need to keep track of time? If students lived in ancient times, they probably wouldn't know when their birthday was. How would they feel?

Have students research examples of timepieces from history, starting with the sun and progressing to modern electronic clocks, to create a bulletin board collage. Their examples might include moon charts, observatories, calendars, sundials, water clocks, candle clocks, mechanical clocks, hourglasses, pendulums, spring-driven clocks, watches, and digital clocks. Discuss the accuracy of each timepiece. For example, a sundial can measure hours but not one minute. A water clock can measure minutes but not one second. Then have students work in cooperative groups to do the activity on reproducible page 42.

Answers

The rate of dripping is not constant. As water drains from a container, the water pressure decreases and the dripping slows. Thus, the marks are not evenly spaced. What variables make a water clock inaccurate? Spillage, evaporation, inexact or changing size of holes, extreme temperature, size or shape of the containers, number of containers, and so on.

> **"The great difference between young America and Old Fogy is the result of discoveries, inventions, and improvements."**
> —Abraham Lincoln

DISCUSS: Why did America become the leading country for inventions? How and why did being a young country make a difference?

💡 Extension

Have students create various types of hourglasses—one minute, two minutes, five minutes, etc. Ship captains used hourglasses to navigate by dead reckoning (estimating distance by speed and time elapsed). How can students control the flow of sand? What variables make hourglasses inaccurate? Experiment with other substances such as rice or salt. This illustration shows one way students might make a simple hourglass using easy-to-find materials.

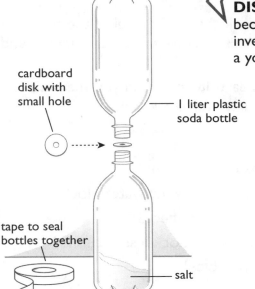

cardboard disk with small hole

l liter plastic soda bottle

tape to seal bottles together

salt

Make a Water Clock

Water clocks measure the passage of time—how many minutes go by. Ancient Egyptians, Romans, and Greeks relied on them. How do they work? Find out here.

What You Need

2 clear, flexible plastic cups
Ruler
Masking tape
Ballpoint pen
Pitcher of water
Measuring cup
Paper towels
Watch with a second hand

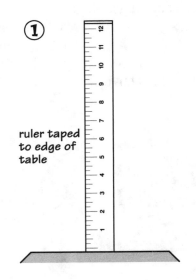

① ruler taped to edge of table

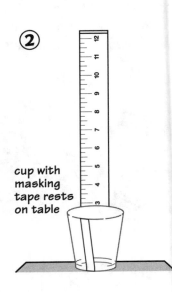

② cup with masking tape rests on table

What to Do

1. Tape one end of the ruler to the side of a table. The ruler should stand up straight and secure.

2. Place a strip of masking tape from top to bottom on one of the cups. Set this cup on the table next to the ruler.

3. Use a ballpoint pen to poke a hole in the bottom of the other cup. Tape this cup onto the ruler a few inches above the first cup.

4. Pour 1 cup (250 mL) of water into the top cup and begin timing 30 seconds.

5. When 30 seconds are up, mark the water level of the bottom cup. Mark it again after one minute, one and a half minutes, and so on until the cup is full.

6. Empty the water into the measuring cup. Can you measure exactly one minute with your water clock?

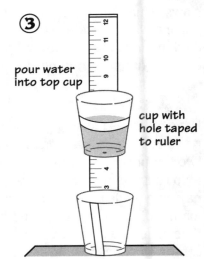

③ pour water into top cup

cup with hole taped to ruler

Think About It

1. Why aren't the marked lines evenly spaced?

2. How does the size of the hole affect your water clock?

3. How does the height of the top cup affect it?

4. What variables (factors) make your clock less accurate?

5. How can you change these variables?

Speedy Inventions

Students read a graph that shows how inventions dramatically changed transportation travel times through history.

Curriculum
Connections
✓ Social Studies
✓ Math

Background

The supersonic (faster than sound) Concorde jet can cross the Atlantic in three hours. The space shuttle can orbit Earth in 90 minutes. But what makes these times truly impressive is a comparison with transportation times of the past. Ships of the Age of Exploration (15th to 17th centuries) took about a month to cross the Atlantic and several years to circumnavigate the globe. Clipper ships and steamships of the 18th and 19th centuries cut the time in half, to roughly two weeks.

Similar dramatic reductions in travel time took place on land. Ancient people relied almost entirely on beast, boat, or their own two feet. Travel at sea was faster than travel over land. Horse-drawn vehicles facilitated travel to the next town or castle but were still painfully slow on long journeys. As machines replaced horses, steam-driven and gas-driven vehicles made coast-to-coast travel easier and faster.

What changes did these advances bring? Perhaps the biggest effect was an explosion of world trade. Goods from every corner of the world could be shipped or, later, flown to every other corner. Cultural ideas, technology, and lifestyles diffused around the world or were assimilated into other cultures. In short, the world became a much smaller place.

Lesson Ideas

The activity on reproducible page 44 compares how long it would take to go 10 miles at various points in history and in various vehicles. Students must plot the times horizontally on the bar graph and then answer questions.

Advanced math students can calculate the times using the speed-time-distance formula: speed = distance divided by time. For this exercise, write the formula as follows: distance divided by speed = time. For example: If you walk 2 miles per hour, how long will it take you to go 10 miles? 10 miles ÷ 2 mph = 5 hours. Multiply by 60 to convert hours into minutes: 5 hours × 60 minutes per hour = 300 minutes.

Answers

Travel Times Human-pulled wagon, 300 min.; Horse-pulled coach, 30 min.; Railroad, 24 min.; Bicycle, 50 min.; Stanley Steamer car, 24 min.; Motorcar, about 14 min.; Minivan, 10 min.; High-speed train, 3 min. **1.** horse-pulled coach **2.** bicycle **3.** 8 times faster **4.** 100 times faster

💡 Extension

Have students calculate how long it would have taken them to get to school at key dates in history, using the speeds on the graph. They can estimate the mileage from home to school by using a local map or by asking a bus driver or other adult to help them read an odometer. For those less than one mile from school, use feet per minute instead of miles per hour (multiply by 5280 and then divide by 60).

Name _____

Speedy Inventions

How long does it take to you to get to school? How long would it take you if you lived in the 16th century? Or the 19th century? For each vehicle below, plot the time it takes to travel 10 miles. Color in the bar. Then answer the questions.

Year	Vehicle	Typical Speed
1550	Human-pulled wagon	2 mph
1785	Horse-pulled coach	20 mph
1830	Railroad	25 mph
1870	Bicycle	12 mph
1897	Stanley Steamer car	25 mph
1923	Motorcar	42 mph
1990	Minivan	60 mph
2000	High-speed train	200 mph

Time to Travel 10 Miles

0 20 40 60 80 100 120 140 160 180 200 220 240 260 280 300 320

Time in Minutes

Questions

1. What vehicle takes three times longer than a minivan? _____

2. What nineteenth-century invention is slower than earlier inventions listed? _____

3. How much faster is the high-speed train than the railroad? _____

4. How much faster is the high-speed train than a human-pulled wagon? _____

Tool Time

Students examine illustrations of unidentified tools of the past and brainstorm possible uses for the inventions.

Background

Before the Industrial Revolution, people generally made their own tools. Though blacksmiths might have forged a cutting blade, the purchaser made his or her own custom handle. Each tool was made-to-order for a specific task, but it often ended up serving many purposes. Meat hooks doubled as well hooks (for grabbing stored food), for example. An isolated farmer—no car, no phone—had to make do with what was available.

Lesson Ideas

Distribute reproducible page 46. Divide students into teams and have each team concentrate on one of the eight inventions on the page. Tell students that this is a creative exercise. They don't have to guess the real uses of the tools; the idea is to imagine possible uses. To demonstrate, show students an unidentified kitchen tool such as a garlic press, a device for removing pineapple eyes, or an apple slicer. Brainstorm possible uses. Have each team draw and label a picture of its best idea.

> **"A tool is but an extension of a man's hand."**
> —*Henry Ward Beecher*

DISCUSS: What tools extend the abilities of our bodies—our reach, our strength, our speed, or our accuracy, for example?

Answers

1. Oil lamp: A wick draws oil from the chamber of the shell to the tip. When lit, the wick burns for hours. **2.** Spindle: As it twirls, thread wraps around it. The stone makes it twirl longer. **3.** Try square: The bronze triangle helps builders make square corners. **4.** Microscope: The pin holds the object. The lens is the circle in the center. **5.** Lightning rod: When set on a roof, the rod attracts lightning. A wire (not shown) carries the electricity safely to the ground.
6. Well hook: When attached to a rope, the well hook lifts objects out of a well. Before refrigerators, people stored food in wells to keep it cool. **7.** Scorper: It scoops out the insides of tree trunks to make canoes. **8.** Can opener: The can opener was invented decades after the tin can first appeared! Prior to its invention, people used knives to pry open cans.

💡 Extension

Cartoons such as the *Flintstones,* the *Jetsons,* and *Roadrunner* are rich sources of invention ideas. Students can keep a list of inventions for a particular show, draw and describe them, and then explain why they would or wouldn't work outside "Toon Town." Two video resources are *Flintstones: Wacky Inventions* and *Stone Age Racer: Wacky Inventions on the Move* (Turner Video, 1994). Challenge students to invent "Stone Age" computers, photocopiers, and drinking fountains.

Tool Time

Before factories, people invented and made their own tools. They often found many uses for these homemade tools. Choose one of the tools below. Then imagine and describe at least three ways to use it.

Example

1. 50,000 B.C., France

◆ Hanging plant holder for small plants
◆ Well dipper for bringing up water
◆ Doorbell: Blow in the shell to announce your arrival.

2. 7000 B.C., Mesopotamia (now Iraq)

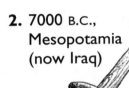

3. 2600 B.C., Egypt

4. 1683, Netherlands

5. 1752, United States

6. 1770, United States

7. 1820, United States

8. 1855, England

Invention #____   Possible Uses:

1. _____

2. _____

3. _____

4. _____

5. _____

Great Moments, Great Messages

Students create a great message for the very first telephone call. Then they write a speech about the moment in history.

Background

Most inventions succeed after years, decades, and even lifetimes of hard work. Before every success are failures—models that didn't quite work or didn't work well enough. History tends to downplay hard work in favor of the few seconds when an inventor can finally say "Eureka!" These snapshots in time grow in importance along with the invention and often take on mythical proportions.

Lesson Ideas

What does it mean when someone shouts "Eureka!"? When might you hear or say this word? The Greek scientist Archimedes shouted "Eureka!" when he discovered a way to measure the purity of gold. In Greek the word means "I have found it."

Reproducible page 48 presents several "Eureka!" moments in the lives of famous inventors. But instead of saying "Eureka!" they chose other words. What would students say? Remind them that their words will be remembered for centuries to come.

Collect all the messages into a booklet and include students' speeches about how they felt at such a great moment.

> **"Out of every ten innovations attempted, nine will end up in silliness. The tenth . . . will show little new in the end."**
> —*Antonio Machade*

WRITE: Give students the first sentence of the quotation. Ask them to complete the idea. Compare their thoughts with Machade's pessimistic view of inventions.

💡 Extension

Collect famous quotes from inventors, starting with the ones in this book. Have students sort the quotes into subject categories and assemble them into a booklet. Students might also want to invent a "Who Said It?" trivia game or match-up activity in which classmates complete the second half of a quotation.

> **"If I have seen further it is by standing on the shoulders of giants."**
> —*Sir Isaac Newton*

DISCUSS: How does this statement apply to inventors? Does it apply to all inventors?

Great Moments, Great Messages

The first telephone

Who was the first person to make a telephone call? The inventor, of course. Alexander Graham Bell had only one person to call—his assistant in the next room. But that call went down in history. What famous words would *you* have said if you were in Bell's shoes?

1. Write your great message here: _____

_____

2. After your great moment in history, you have to give a speech. Who is present? What do you say to them? How will your invention change their lives? Write your speech here. Use the back of this page if you need more room.

_____

_____

_____

_____

_____

💡 Four Historical Messages

"Come here, Watson. I want you."

The first words spoken on a telephone, in 1876, by inventor Alexander Graham Bell

"One small step for man. One giant leap for mankind."

The first moon-to-Earth broadcast, in 1969, by astronaut Neil Armstrong

"Mr. Marconi sends Mr. Branly his respectful compliments for the wireless [message] across the Channel, this beautiful result being due in part to the remarkable work of Mr. Branly."

The first wireless (radio) message sent over the English Channel, in 1899, by inventor Gugliemo Marconi

"Yankee Doodle Dandy," whistled.

The first magnetic recording (tape recording), in 1937, by Marvin Camras

The Great All-Time Inventions Game

Goal

Correctly place the most invention cards on The Great All-Time Inventions timeline. Students don't have to know the exact dates of the inventions. They simply place them in chronological order relative to one another.

Players

4 to 6 players or teams plus 1 nonplayer to act as game monitor

Materials

The Great All-Time Inventions game board (See poster bound in the back of this book.)

32 Invention Cards (reproducible pages 51 and 52)

32 colored tokens, such as counters or buttons (one color for each team or player)

Reference List (page 50)

cardboard

paste

scissors

Preparation

1. To make the Invention cards sturdier, paste the reproducible pages onto cardboard. When the paste dries, cut out the cards. To extend the life of the poster and the cards, laminate them.

2. Place the game board on a table.

3. Shuffle the playing cards and deal them evenly to each team or player. Place leftover cards on the game board in their correct positions. (See Reference List.)

4. Assign each team or player a token color.

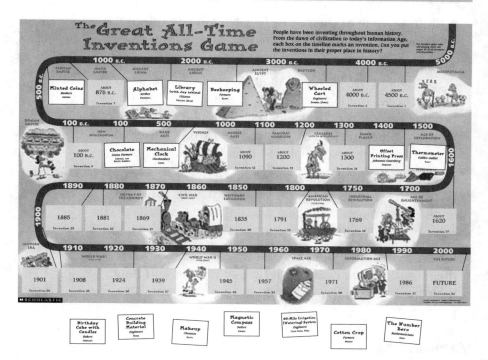

Rules for Playing

1. Students read their cards. Each card names an invention, its inventor(s), and where it was invented. These clues and the pictures on the game board can help narrow down a time period for most of the inventions. Also prompt students with questions:

   ◆ What is the purpose of the invention?

   ◆ Is there a time in history when having the invention was important?

   ◆ What technology had to exist to make the invention possible?

   ◆ When was the country of origin in existence?

   ◆ Is the invention related to any other inventions on the game board?

2. Teams or players take turns placing any one of their cards on the timeline and cover the cards with their colored token. The game monitor keeps the game board orderly.

3. Players will place some cards on the wrong spots. That's okay for now—it's part of the game. On each turn, before playing a card, players can make two moves:

   ◆ Shift any one of their already-played cards (but not opponents' cards) to another spot on the timeline.

   ◆ Challenge an opponent's card, but only if it's on the spot where the player is about to play. The game monitor checks the Reference List to see which card (if either) belongs on the spot and then places the correct card on the timeline. Any incorrect card or cards go back to the team that played them. The turn is over.

4. As soon as all cards have been played, the game is over. To find the winner, the game monitor checks the places of all the cards and eliminates any that are incorrect. The team or player with the most correct cards wins.

5. Collect and shuffle the cards for a new round or affix them to the game board with tape or Funtak and hang the completed poster as a reference for your unit on inventions.

Variations

1. Play cooperatively as a class. Have students work together to figure out the correct order of all the cards—like a jigsaw puzzle. When they are done, check their timeline and remove and return all incorrect cards. Have students find new spots for the incorrect cards. Check their work again and remove incorrect cards. Continue until the timeline is correct.

2. Make a mini-timeline game for individuals. Choose or make 12 cards per set. Challenge students to arrange their set in order. When they believe they have all the cards in place, they can check them against the Reference List.

3. Include a research component. Have students work in teams and set a time limit during which they can refer to reference materials to answer the questions.

4. Make the game harder by narrowing the time period to a century; by concentrating on a theme such as transportation, clothing, appliances, tools, or toys; or by using more cards. You don't need a new poster. Players can simply arrange the new cards in order on a table. Or re-create the timeline on the game board on a large sheet of butcher paper.

Reference List
(in chronological order)

1. Cotton Crop: ca. 4500 B.C.
2. Makeup: ca. 4000 B.C.
3. Wheeled Cart: ca. 3500 B.C.
4. Beekeeping: ca. 2500 B.C.
5. Library: ca. 1700 B.C.
6. Alphabet: ca. 1000 B.C.
7. The Number Zero: ca. 876 B.C.
8. Minted Coins: ca. 600 B.C.
9. Concrete: ca. 100 B.C.
10. Chocolate: ca. A.D. 100
11. Mechanical Clock: ca. A.D. 725
12. Magnetic Compass: ca. A.D. 1090
13. Birthday Cake: ca. 1200
14. Irrigation System: ca. 1300
15. Printing Press: ca. 1450
16. Thermometer: 1593
17. Submarine: ca. 1620
18. Steam Engine: 1769
19. Metric System: 1791
20. Revolver: 1835
21. Coast-to-Coast Railroad: 1869
22. Elevated Railway: 1881
23. Gas-Powered Automobile: 1885
24. Radio: 1901
25. Factory Assembly Line: 1908
26. Frozen Food: 1924
27. Jet Plane: 1939
28. Atomic Bomb: 1945
29. Satellite: 1957
30. Hit Video Game: 1971
31. Robot Submarine: 1986
32. Micro-Robot Surgeons: Future

Concrete Building Material
Engineers
ROME

Cotton Crop
Farmers
MEXICO

Makeup
Chemists
EGYPT

Wheeled Cart
Engineers
SUMERIA (SYRIA)

Beekeeping
Farmers
EGYPT

Library (with clay tablets)
Citizens
CHALDEA (IRAQ)

Alphabet
Scribes
PHOENICIA

The Number Zero
Mathematicians
INDIA

Minted Coins
Bankers
ASSYRIA

Chocolate
Cocoa Farmers
CENTRAL AND SOUTH AMERICA

Mechanical Clock
Clockmakers
CHINA

Magnetic Compass
Sailors
ARABIA

Birthday Cake with Candles
Bakers
GERMANY

46-Mile Irrigation (Watering) System
Engineers
CHAN CHAN, PERU

Offset Printing Press
Johannes Gutenberg
GERMANY

Thermometer
Galileo Galilei
ITALY

Leather, Oar-Powered Submarine *Cornelius Drebbel* HOLLAND	**Steam Engine** *James Watt* GREAT BRITAIN	**Metric System** *Revolutionary Government* FRANCE	**Revolver** (six-shooter) *Samuel Colt* UNITED STATES
Coast-to-Coast Railroad *Union Pacific* UNITED STATES	**Elevated Railway** *Mary Walton* UNITED STATES	**Gas-Powered Automobile** *Gottlieb Daimler and Karl Benz* GERMANY	**Radio** *Gugliemo Marconi* ITALY
Factory Assembly Line *Henry Ford* UNITED STATES	**Frozen Food** *Clarence Birdseye* UNITED STATES	**Mechanical Jet Plane** (Heinkel He178) *Hans von Ohain and Ernst Heinkel* GERMANY	**Atomic Bomb** (Trinity) *The Manhattan Project* UNITED STATES
Satellite (Sputnik) *Soviet Space Agency* SOVIET UNION	**Hit Video Game** (Pong) *Noland Bushnel* UNITED STATES	**Robot Submarine** (Jason) *Woods Hole Oceanographic Institution* UNITED STATES	**Micro-Robot Surgeons** (to enter and unclog blood vessels) *Engineers* UNITED STATES

True or Fraud?

Students use logic and basic science to decide if inventions are real or fake. They then play either the role of inventors hoping to sell an invention or of citizens who must decide if a too-good-to-be-true invention is legitimate.

Curriculum Connections
✓ Social Studies
✓ Language Arts
✓ Science
✓ Art
✓ Drama
✓ Creative Thinking

Background

Since the beginning of civilization, hucksters have conned gullible or ignorant citizens into buying false inventions. Some of yesterday's far-fetched machines are now possible. Others are not. For example:

◆ Alchemists from Mesopotamia to medieval Europe claimed to know a secret recipe for changing lead into gold. They didn't. But in the Atomic Age, scientists discovered that elements can and do change through radioactive decay. However, the cost of making this happen quickly would far exceed the value of any resulting gold.

◆ Many inventors claim to have built "perpetual motion machines," which supposedly run forever with no additional input of energy. Such machines are impossible, thanks to the law of conservation of energy. The amount of energy always stays the same. Some energy goes toward overcoming friction. So less and less energy is kinetic (the energy of motion). The machine inevitably slows and stops. The Patent Office flatly refuses any patent applications for perpetual motion machines.

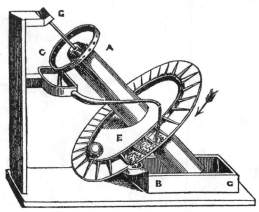

◆ Unscrupulous inventors of the 18th and 19th centuries created machines that appeared to play chess. One famous hoax used a machine with a smallish intelligent human hidden inside. Today's computers not only play chess, a few have even beaten human grandmasters!

◆ Snake oil peddlers sold—and still sell—bogus cure-all potions or miracle beauty products. They often bolted out of town before anyone could catch on. Con artists are still making the same false boasts in ads and on product labels. There's no single "cure-all" medicine. Different diseases require different treatments.

◆ During times of drought, so-called rainmakers claimed that elaborate machines would make clouds burst wide open. Their fees were exorbitant—$10,000 or even more—but desperate farmers sometimes paid them. Rain would eventually fall on its own (as the rainmaker well knew), but either way, the con artist was long gone with the loot. Today, airplanes can seed clouds with a chemical called silver iodide that forces raindrops to fall. But rain clouds must be present for this process to work.

Lesson Ideas

Divide the class into six groups and discuss some of the bogus claims and hoaxes of past centuries. Would students have been duped? Have each group complete the activity on reproducible page 55. Emphasize that they may not know some of the answers, but neither did consumers when presented with these "inventions." They should draw on logic, common sense, and the collective science knowledge of the group to make the best educated guess possible.

> "I think there is a world market for about five computers."
> —*Thomas Watson*

PREDICT: Watson, the founder of IBM, made this bold but very wrong prediction before personal computers hit the scene. What future prediction about computers would students make today?

Assign five of the six groups to be traveling inventors of the 19th century. These groups—and these groups alone—get copies of reproducible page 56. Each group should select or make up an invention that's sure to sell. They will need a model that works—or appears to work—and a sales pitch. They must also prepare a short written description of their invention to submit to the townspeople—the students in the sixth group.

The townspeople use the written descriptions to research the inventions and prepare hard questions to expose any scientific impossibilities. After the inventors present their wares and the townspeople ask their questions, the townspeople should vote on whether to make inventors rich by buying their inventions or imprison them for fraud.

💡 Extensions

Ask students to keep their eyes peeled for bogus products on the market today. What claims sound too good to be true? What products have they tried that don't work or don't work well? Ripe areas to explore include beauty products, diet schemes, cleaning products, and pest-control devices. For example, electronic flea collars that emit a high-frequency sound don't work because fleas simply can't hear them. Yet people buy them.

Modern machines seem to work "like magic," but they are based on solid science. You press a button; the TV turns on. Press another button; your dinner is cooked. Have students take apart, study, and draw the inner workings of an old, inexpensive, or broken invention: flashlight, stapler, pencil sharpener, wind-up toy, VCR, vacuum, remote control, tape recorder, toaster, telephone, camera, and so on. Scour garage sales, thrift stores, flea markets, basements, and curbsides for materials. The *Exploratorium Home Laboratory II: Hands-On Science Fun for Families* (3601 Lyon Street, San Francisco, California 94123) is a good resource.

In his book *Inventor's Workshop* (Fearon, 1981), Alan McCormack uses magicians' tricks to teach students how to think like scientists and inventors. For example, suppose you put chocolate kisses in a box, and chocolate milk pours out. What's inside the box? Students know that it can't really be magic, so there must be a scientific solution.

True or Fraud?

Which of these inventions could really work? Which ones are frauds—or fakes? Circle your answer and explain how the invention might work or why it can't possibly work.

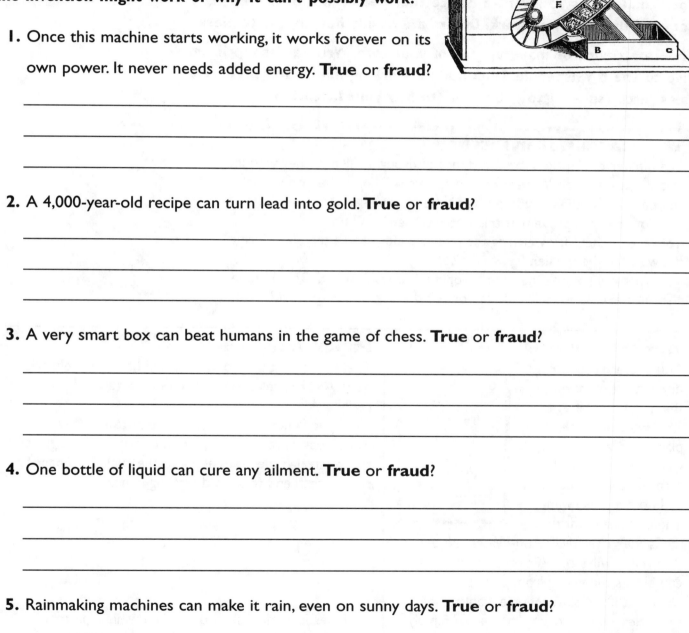

1. Once this machine starts working, it works forever on its own power. It never needs added energy. **True** or **fraud**?

_____

_____

_____

2. A 4,000-year-old recipe can turn lead into gold. **True** or **fraud**?

_____

_____

_____

3. A very smart box can beat humans in the game of chess. **True** or **fraud**?

_____

_____

_____

4. One bottle of liquid can cure any ailment. **True** or **fraud**?

_____

_____

_____

5. Rainmaking machines can make it rain, even on sunny days. **True** or **fraud**?

_____

_____

_____

True or Fraud Invention Ideas

Your challenge is to invent a device that people will buy. Some of these devices work. Others are frauds but appear to work.

Choose a device or make up one of your own. Write a description to give to the townspeople. Then build a working model and prepare a sales pitch (speech) to get people to buy your invention.

The Magic Water Pitcher

The pitcher can "make water" in times of drought. Fill a pitcher with ice water and wait a bit. Water vapor in the air will condense into water and bead up on the outside of the pitcher.

How can you prove that this water is "new" and not just water from the pitcher? Try weighing the pitcher before and after. Try coloring the water in the pitcher. Try what else?

What will you tell the townspeople if it doesn't work? Do you have a science excuse—a scientific reason for the device not to work?

Anti-Water

Anti-Water keeps things dry instead of making them wet—or does it?

Try it: Take a clear plastic cup and tape or glue a tissue inside. Then turn the cup upside down and hold it underwater. The tissue stays dry!

Is the water *really* Anti-Water? Nope. Any water will work. Air pressure inside the cup blocks the water from getting inside.

What if the townspeople want to see this "trick" with ordinary tap water? Simply tilt the cup to allow bubbles out and water in. The ordinary water will appear to be a failure.

Paper Telephone

Telephones cost a lot of money and have fancy electric parts. A cheap telephone made of paper should sell really well!

Try it: Punch a small hole in the bottom of two paper cups. Thread each end of a 6-foot (3-m) length of string through the holes and into the cups. Tie a paper clip on each end to keep the string in place.

Does it work? Talk into one cup while a partner listens in the other. How far apart can you hear each other? How can you make your invention look like a "real" telephone?

In the Year 2121

Students research the advances of an invention over decades or centuries. They then project improvements and innovations for the future in drawings and descriptive prose.

Curriculum Connections

✓ Social Studies
✓ Language Arts
✓ Art

Background

In the Motor City—Detroit, Michigan—auto fans celebrated the 100th anniversary of the car in 1996. (See the November 1996 issue of *American Heritage* for a retrospective.) Few of the early designers could have envisioned today's road wonders—fully automatic, electronic, sleek and sporty. What will the next 100 years bring in car design? Each year, automakers showcase concept cars of the future. Few concept cars ever make it to manufacturing, but the ideas and innovations are what propel the industry forward.

Lesson Ideas

Almost all inventions are improvements on things past. Do students agree? Can they think of a recent invention that is totally original? Ask students to describe the changes in the automobiles pictured on reproducible page 59. Which changes made the cars run better? Which changes were for fashion only? For example:

◆ The first cars just had to work—no frills, no speed, no extra power.

◆ In the early 20th century, automakers needed a design they could copy over and over for little money. The Model T and its sisters filled the bill.

> "I invented nothing new. I simply assembled into a car the discoveries of other men behind whom were centuries of work.... So it is with every new thing."
> —Henry Ford

RESEARCH: What other inventors and inventions contributed to the modern automobile?

◆ Cars in the 1940s began to take on luxuries. Power and speed were important, but drivers also wanted cars that were easy to drive.

◆ In the late 1950s, cars had exaggerated tail fins and lots of chrome—a fashion statement. The small, boxy cars of the 1970s were designed to save fuel during the "energy crisis."

◆ Cars of the 1990s emphasize safety features such as air bags. Today, more car buyers have families and so worry about safety.

What will car buyers of the 21st century look for in an automobile? Consider these projections:

◆ Our population is aging. More car buyers will be senior citizens.

◆ We may experience a fuel shortage again. Or alternative fuels such as methane and natural gas may gradually replace gasoline.

◆ Solar and electric cars may become more practical.

◆ Computers will continue their rapid advancement in speed, memory, and features such as voice recognition.

How else might our society change? How will our automobiles change? Have students draw a design for the car of the future—a 2121 Ford Futura, for example. Another approach: Split students into teams. The first team designs a "car of the future" for 2020, including a description of features. They then hand this design to the second team, who must improve it and add innovations for the year 2040. Continue passing the designs to the "next generation" until the last team has completed its drawing. Hang the drawings in a line and discuss the progression of ideas.

2121 FORD FUTURA

satellite access for tracking and TV

turbine engine runs on water

lights turn on automatically after dark

flat tires automatically reinflate

💡 Extension

Create a timeline of future inventions from the present to the year 2121. The inventions can center around these projected events:

◆ a moon colony of antlike robots that will mine our only satellite for rocket fuel ingredients

◆ a human mission to Mars followed by a human colony of scientists and terraformers (experts in converting "dead" planets into livable ones)

◆ cures for genetic diseases such as cancer and cystic fibrosis and vaccines for deadly viral diseases such as AIDS and Ebola

◆ cloning (genetic copying) of plants and simple animals

◆ overpopulation of the planet

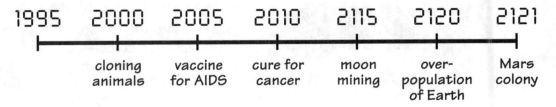

1995	2000	2005	2010	2115	2120	2121
	cloning animals	vaccine for AIDS	cure for cancer	moon mining	over-population of Earth	Mars colony

For each event, ask students to brainstorm what inventions will be necessary or will result from the event and how each event will change existing inventions and lifestyles. Resources such as *The Futurist* can provide clues and ideas. Check your public library for *Encyclopedia of the Future* edited by George Thomas Kurian and Graham T. T. Molitor (Macmillan, 1996).

In the Year 2121

How have cars changed in the last 100 years? How will they keep changing?

Look at the designs of the past. Then draw a car design for the year 2121 on the back of this page. Describe your car's features.

English Steam Car, 1784

Horseless, open, and basic

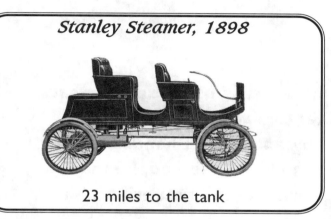

Stanley Steamer, 1898

23 miles to the tank

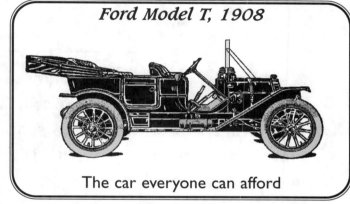

Ford Model T, 1908

The car everyone can afford

Packard Speedster, 1930

Luxury, style, and lots of wind

Chevrolet Impala, 1959

Souped-up tail fins and chrome

Volkswagen Beetle, 1973

Good gas mileage and a low price,
but ugly as a bug

Ford Taurus, 1996

Sporty but safe with built-in air bags

Inventive Thinking and Creating

We are all inventors. Human nature tells us to tinker, create, and improve. But no two inventors work alike.

Thomas Edison had little schooling and took a hands-on approach to inventing. With his "cut-and-try" method, he made model after model, testing and improving each one until he hit upon a working prototype.

Leonardo da Vinci's tanks never rolled and his airplane never flew. Instead of models, Leonardo made detailed drawings.

The activities and projects in this section challenge students to explore a variety of invention approaches: creative thinking, problem solving, teamwork, the scientific method, and just plain tinkering. They also introduce the noncreative part of inventing—market surveys, budgeting and costs, and writing a legal patent.

My Uncle Dan

Students read a poem about an inventor of ridiculous things. Then they generate creative ideas of their own and express them in descriptive prose or poetry and art.

Background

Imagineering means engineering and inventing in your mind. Without worldly constraints such as the laws of physics, anything is possible. Utility, reason, and common sense don't apply.

What good is imagineering? Ask any science fiction writer. (Also see "(Science) Fiction or Fact?" on page 21.) Freeing the mind to explore impossible or useless gadgets can lead to breakthrough inventions of the future. Innovations such as rocketing to the moon, cloning cells, a human-powered aircraft, artificial organs, wrist radios (a fictional predecessor of cell phones), and wiping out a disease such as smallpox started as far-fetched dreams before inventors finally realized them. Here are a two more examples:

"Imagination is more important than knowledge."
—*Albert Einstein*

DISCUSS: Do you agree?

◆ Renaissance artist and inventor Leonard da Vinci imagineered dozens of new gadgets and vehicles (see "One-Man Invention Convention," page 62). He drew detailed schematics of these machines but didn't have the technology actually to build them.

◆ Stone Age drawings in France show animals combined in strange forms— the horns of a deer, face of an owl, ears of a wolf, forelegs of a bear, tail of a horse, and back legs of a human. While today's scientists can't (and probably wouldn't want to) create such fantastical creatures, they can transfer genetic material from one organism to another. A mouse with human cancer genes will develop a tumor, for example.

Lesson Ideas

Hand out reproducible page 63. Ask students to stand in a row and each recite two lines of the poem in turn. While reciting their lines, invite students to act out the words in mime—bounce an imaginary watch off the floor or drink from the imaginary bottomless glass, for example.

Next, have students complete reproducible page 64. List adjectives for Uncle Dan on the chalkboard. Discuss and mark which ones are positive and which ones are negative. Is it worthwhile to invent or imagine things that can't really exist or be used? Why or why not?

If students are stuck for ideas for an Uncle Dan–like invention, trigger their creativity by asking them to take an object at random from a bag. Focusing on this object, they should write a list of words that describe or are associated with it.

💡 Extension

Today's science fiction contains the seeds of tomorrow's inventions. Generate a class list of futuristic gadgets, gizmos, and vehicles from popular movies and books. For example, *Star Trek* introduced warp speed (faster than light) transporters that "beam" people around and replicators that create objects such as food by rearranging molecules. Many of these machines are scientifically impossible or far-fetched. But ask students to imagine how machines like these would change their future lives on Earth.

One-Man Invention Convention

The great artist Leonardo da Vinci (1452–1519) is also famous as an inventor, even though he never built working models of many of his ideas. Here are just a few of Leonardo's ahead-of-his-time designs:

- anemometer (measures wind speed)
- automatic roaster
- coin stamper
- cord drives (led to today's belt-driven machines)
- device to measure the strength of wires
- diving suit
- dredge (clears swamps)
- monkey wrench
- movable cam (lopsided cylinder that moves with a rocking motion and is now crucial to many machines)
- needle maker
- paper feeder for printing presses
- pedometer (measures steps taken while walking)
- pipe borer
- pliers
- prefabricated house
- pump for deep wells or mines
- ratchet jack
- reciprocating saw
- spring-driven car (later a model for toy cars)
- wooden tank

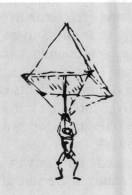

Leonardo da Vinci made many attempts to solve the problem of human flight. He designed many flying machines that used muscular power and parachutes.

My Uncle Dan

My Uncle Dan's an inventor, you may think that's very fine.
You may wish he was your Uncle instead of being mine—
If he wanted he could make a watch that bounces when it drops,
He could make a helicopter out of string and bottle tops
Or any useful thing you can't get in the shops.

But Uncle Dan has other ideas:
The bottomless glass for ginger beers,
The toothless saw that's safe for the tree,
A special word for a spelling bee
(Like Lionocerangoutangadder),
Or the roll-uppable rubber ladder,
The mystery pie that bites when it's bit—
My Uncle Dan invented it.

My Uncle Dan sits in his den inventing night and day.
His eyes peer from his hair and beard like mice from a load of hay.
And does he make the shoes that will go on walks without your feet?
A shrinker to shrink instantly the elephants you meet?
A carver that just carves from the air steaks cooked and ready to eat?

No, no he has other intentions—
Only perfectly useless inventions:
Glassless windows (they never break),
A medicine to cure the earthquake,
The unspillable screwed-down cup,
The stairs that go neither down nor up,
The door you simply paint on a wall—
Uncle Dan invented them all.

—Ted Hughes

My Uncle Dan Questions

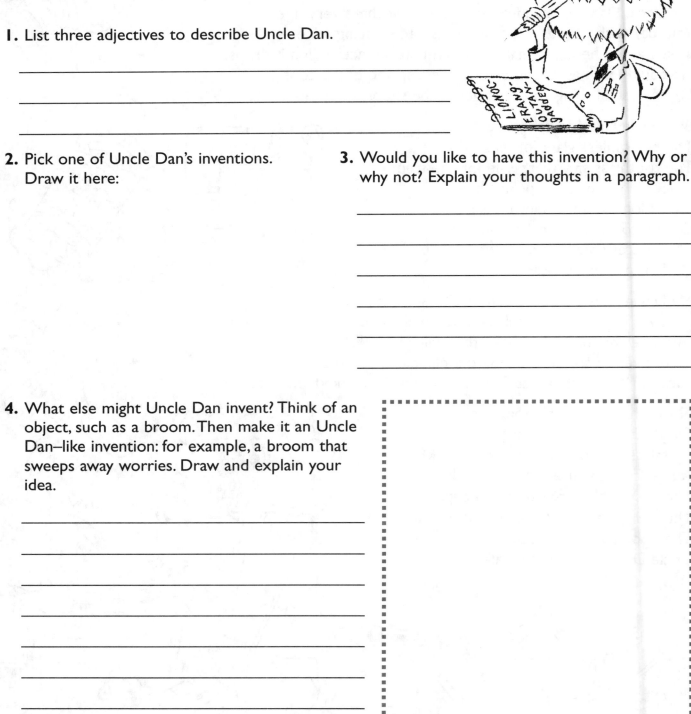

1. List three adjectives to describe Uncle Dan.

_____

_____

_____

2. Pick one of Uncle Dan's inventions. Draw it here:

3. Would you like to have this invention? Why or why not? Explain your thoughts in a paragraph.

_____

_____

_____

_____

_____

_____

4. What else might Uncle Dan invent? Think of an object, such as a broom. Then make it an Uncle Dan–like invention: for example, a broom that sweeps away worries. Draw and explain your idea.

_____

_____

_____

_____

_____

_____

_____

Think Like an Inventor & Are You an Inventor?

Students explore the characteristics of a successful inventor by taking a brief self-assessment quiz and examining a list of guidelines.

Background

Inventors definitely share certain traits—the ability to concentrate, work hard, and ignore detractors, for example. But many of these traits are learned, not innate. Anyone can fine-tune them with practice. Anyone can be an inventor. Consider that finger paintings, new combinations of clothes, and jury-rigged repairs are all inventions.

To create, patent, and market an invention doesn't take genius, but it does take all or most of the steps on the "How to Think Like an Inventor" reproducible (page 67). Though some inventors (Leonardo da Vinci, Albert Einstein) were geniuses, the majority are ordinary people who see a problem and solve it.

> **"A problem is a chance for you to do your best."**
> —Duke Ellington

WRITE: Describe a problem that you solved recently.

Lesson Ideas

The self-assessment quiz on reproducible page 68 echoes the list of qualities of an inventor. Question 1 deals with a student's willingness to tackle a problem head-on with hard work (b) and not give up (a) or avoid the problem (c). It takes self-confidence to risk failure or "losing."

Question 2 asks about the student's flexibility (b and c) and willingness to ignore conventions (c). Opening the mind to new ideas and new ways of doing or seeing things is creativity in a nutshell. Not that following a recipe is a *bad* thing. In fact, being able both to follow recipes *and* create new recipes is the best of both worlds.

Question 3 covers the inventor's axiom that failures are opportunities to succeed (a), and that mistakes and other obstacles stand in your way only if you let them (b and c).

Question 4 addresses the inventor's belief that everything under the sun has *not* already been invented (a). A better mousetrap will always come along. Only people who are open-minded will see it.

> **"Genius is 1 percent inspiration, and 99 percent perspiration."**
> –Thomas Edison

DEBATE: Does an inventor have to be a genius to succeed?

Question 5 acknowledges that all inventors have something to learn. Thomas Edison didn't know much science when he started, but he sure learned fast. A desire to learn (a and c) is even more powerful when paired with a penchant to involve other people, especially experts (c).

Question 6 will ring a bell with all students who have been picked on or made fun of. Inventors ignore detractors (b) and keep walking to their own beat. Naysayers failed to stop NASA from landing on the moon, the Wright Brothers from flying, and the first submarine from submerging (in 1620!).

> **"Always think for yourself and listen to your ideas, even if they sound crazy at first."**
> —*Sarita M. James (student inventor)*
>
> **"An inventor may try hundreds of things that don't work, and that give most people the impression that he is somewhat crazy."**
> –*Marvin Camras*

DISCUSS: How would you respond to someone who said your ideas were crazy?

Solicit real-life examples for each scenario on the quiz. As students describe and draw a typical inventor, watch for evidence of biases—mad scientists, geniuses only, and a lack of women and minorities. Several books provide examples of non-stereotypical inventors (see Resources on page 95); also listed are invention contests open to any student as young as kindergarten.

Have pairs of students choose a message on the "How to Think Like an Inventor" list and create an advertisement to broadcast the message. The ad could be a poster, a videotape, a song, or a combination of media.

💡 Extension

Have each student write a classified ad for inventors. Half the class can pose as companies looking to hire inventors, and the other half can pose as inventors looking for jobs. What are the qualifications? What is the level of experience or education?

Can Students Invent a Better . . .

Pick an item from the list. Think of what's wrong, awkward, boring, or bothersome about it. Then brainstorm ways to improve the item.

housefly trap
alarm clock
burglar alarm
antisnoring device
doll or stuffed animal
back-scratcher
umbrella for rain or sun
theft-proof purse or backpack
exercise machine
eyeglasses
way to get rid of secondhand smoke
camouflage fabric
shark-protection suit

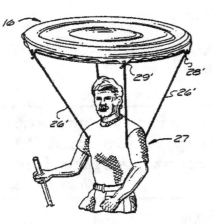

Patent Number 5,076,029: A floating helium disk shades people who work outdoors.

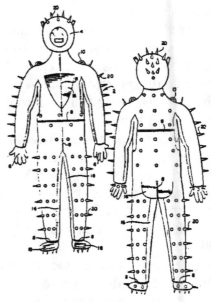

Patent Number 4,833,729: Medieval-style chain mail (steel mesh) made of space-age material keeps shark bites at bay.

How to Think Like an Inventor

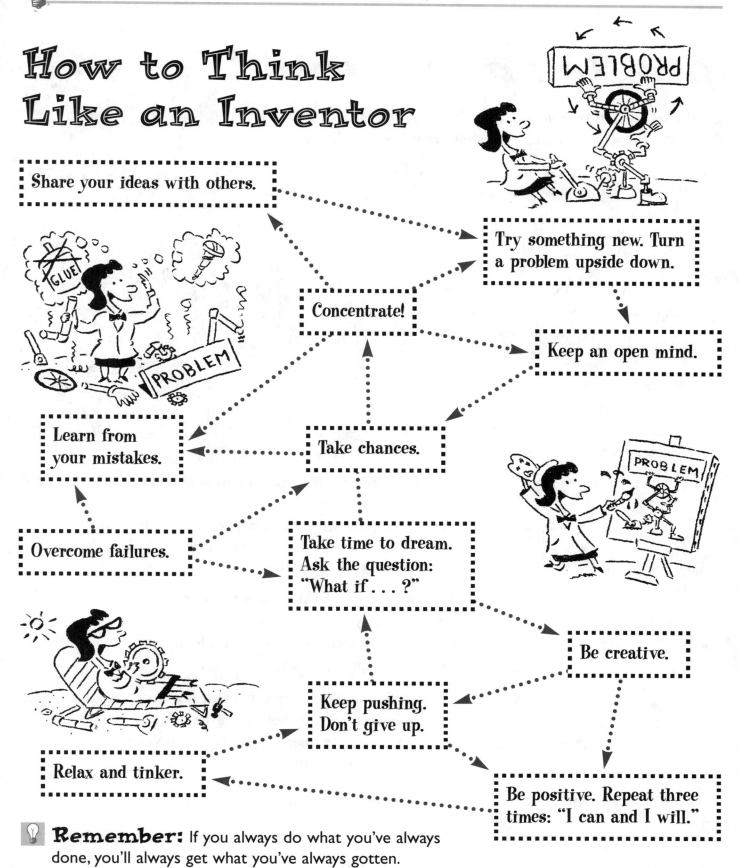

Remember: If you always do what you've always done, you'll always get what you've always gotten.

Are You an Inventor?

Read each situation below.
Circle the answer that best matches what you would do.

1. You are playing soccer. A new kid joins the team.
   She plays your position very, very well. You:
   - **a.** quit.
   - **b.** practice harder.
   - **c.** switch positions.

2. You are making cookies for Halloween. You:
   - **a.** always follow recipes exactly.
   - **b.** follow a recipe but add your own touches.
   - **c.** experiment to make a whole new cookie.

3. Your cookies turn out awful. You:
   - **a.** try to find out why.
   - **b.** throw them out and vow to never bake again.
   - **c.** only make easier recipes from now on.

4. A friend wants to show you a new way to tie your shoes. You:
   - **a.** watch and learn.
   - **b.** let him, but don't really believe his way is better.
   - **c.** tell him people have always tied their shoes a certain way. Why change now?

5. You have never fixed the chain on your bike. You:
   - **a.** try it on your own.
   - **b.** put it off because it seems too hard.
   - **c.** ask a neighbor to show you how.

6. An older kid makes fun of the weird way you play guitar. You:
   - **a.** try harder to copy how other people play.
   - **b.** ignore her and keep playing how you want.
   - **c.** quit or switch instruments.

7. Write three adjectives that could describe an inventor. _____

_____

8. Draw a picture of an inventor on the back of this page.

My Idea Book & Six Rules of Inventing

Students begin keeping an inventor's notebook that includes Thomas Edison's rules for inventing. The first entry is a thinking exercise to begin generating ideas.

Background

Many inventors keep a detailed notebook of ideas, schematics, and data. One reason is to prove that they were the first to come up with an invention. But notebooks serve many purposes: to organize ideas, to remember ideas, as a brainstorming tool, as a record of what went wrong and right, and for posterity.

There are as many approaches to the invention process as there are inventors. A common thread is to scour the world for problems, hang-ups, and needs. Inventions must make some task or object easier, faster, more fun—or just plain better. Even Uncle Dan's far-fetched inventions (page 63) generally fill the bill. A second common requisite is to research the problem, hang-up, or need. Learn the science. Study the market. Take things apart and put them back together again.

Finally, invention guidelines include exercises for brainstorming solutions, refining and sketching the best ideas, and building and testing models to get a working prototype.

> **"The best way to have a good idea is to have lots of ideas."**
> —Linus Pauling
>
> **BRAINSTORM:** How many ways can you catch a fly?

Lesson Ideas

Have students start an Idea Book in a loose-leaf notebook. Hand out reproducible page 71. Tell them to make "Thomas Edison's Six Rules of Inventing" the first page of their Idea Book. As they go through the invention process, they can answer the questions one at a time. Note Edison's emphasis on cooperative teamwork, communication, and record keeping. You may want to establish invention teams early in the process, making sure each team has students with a range of abilities and interests. Designating tasks for each team member need not be a permanent assignment. Encourage teams to rotate leaders, recorders, researchers, and model builders.

"My Invention Idea Book" on reproducible page 70 is a first, easy step toward generating ideas. For more challenge, have each student pull an object at random out of a box. Simple objects work best—pencils, rulers, empty lunch bags, rolls of tape, and so on. An excellent example of this thinking technique is a Web site called "Inventing a New Kind of Pencil (and Eraser)" by Duen Hsi Yen (yen@noogenesis.com).

> **"No idea is a bad idea. Every idea leads to the next idea."**
> —Jamie Lynn Villella (student inventor)
>
> **DISCUSS:** Do you agree?

💡 Extension

Ask students to list in their notebooks things that annoy them, things they'd like to do faster or better, things that other people seem to need, and things that are really popular.

Name _____

My Invention Idea Book

You never know when a bright idea will strike. Like lightning, it could be there one moment and gone the next. That's why inventors record their ideas in a notebook. This page will get you started. First, find any item, such as a ruler, pen, eraser, etc. Then answer the questions.

ITEM: _____

1. What's wrong with this item? List at least three things. _____

_____

_____

_____

2. What would make this item better? List three or more improvements. _____

_____

_____

_____

3. What new use could this item have? List three or more ideas. _____

_____

_____

_____

4. Put the item next to another item that's not related. How could you join the two items into a

single tool or product? _____

_____

_____

_____

5. How would you reinvent the item?
Draw and label a picture of your plan on the back of this page.

Thomas Edison's Six Rules of Inventing

Thomas Edison won 1,093 U.S. patents. He was the first to enter the National Inventors Hall of Fame. So take it from a pro. Here are Edison's six rules to invention success. Read them and think: How can I apply each one to my invention?

Thomas Edison

1. Don't invent useless things.

Who needs your invention? Why? _____

_____

2. Set a goal. Then stick to it.

What is your goal? _____

_____

3. List the steps for reaching your goal. Then follow them.

How do you plan to achieve your goal? _____

_____

4. Share all data with your team of inventors.

Who is on your invention team? What experts will you need? _____

_____

5. Assign each team member a specific job.

What is the job for each member of your team? _____

_____

6. Keep very careful records. That way, you can go back and learn from your mistakes and successes.

What ideas have you had so far? What data have you collected? _____

_____

Think Creatively! & Think Links

To generate ideas for inventions, students choose an ordinary object and think of eight creative new uses for it. They then find common bonds between seemingly unrelated items.

Background

In a general sense, *brainstorming* means "thinking up a list of ideas." But there are more specific definitions that suit the inventing process:

◆ Medium-sized groups brainstorm; individuals, small groups (fewer than 4), and big groups (more than 10) do not.

◆ Brainstormers should make absolutely no judgments; all ideas are accepted and included, no matter how silly or seemingly far-fetched.

◆ The more ideas, the better; don't worry about quality.

◆ The first ideas are usually not the best ones; don't stop too early.

◆ Brainstorming is hard, focused work, not sitting around waiting for lightning to strike.

◆ The goal should be clear and the desired outcome understood by all.

Brainstorming requires creative thinking. Like intelligence, creativity is a part of every human being. We are all intelligent. We are all creative. But we're all intelligent and creative in different ways. Genetic differences aside, we each choose how much, how well, and toward what end to be creative. Developing creativity to its fullest is just like exercising to get in shape. Choosing how to use our creativity is like choosing soccer over bodybuilding.

Thinking exercises can turn a creative person into a highly creative person. Or they can shift a person's creative focus from one field to another. One such technique is called SCAMPER:

Substitute (computer for typewriter)

Combine (Swiss army knife)

Adapt or Adjust (lunar module into a space capsule during *Apollo 13* mission)

Modify or Minify or Magnify (trees into miniature bonsai trees)

Put to New Uses (clear nail polish to stop panty hose runs)

Eliminate or Elaborate (mechanical sewing machine to electronic one)

Reverse or Rearrange (lawn tractors with the deck in front, back, underneath, or to the side)

Lesson Ideas

Having objects on hand, especially old ones that students can reshape and take apart, will make "Think Creatively!" on reproducible page 74 easier. As the time period winds down, students may write in any old thing to complete their lists. There are several ways to avoid this: Don't impose a target number, increase the size of the teams, make this exercise an ongoing one that students can do a few minutes each day or at home, or use the SCAMPER technique (see page 72) to spark ideas.

Teams should write all of their ideas in their Idea Books. Tell each team member to circle and draw his or her favorite idea—the one that seems the most doable, useful, or popular.

"Think Links" on reproducible page 75 have no right or wrong answers. As long as students can explain the similarity between each pair of items on the list, their link is valid. The fun begins when you compare a classroom's worth of links for the same pair of objects. Students will begin to see the objects in many dimensions and from many points of view. For example, the introduction examines a magazine and a bicycle from the point of view of how people use them, their shape and size, why people use them, and the structure of their purpose—a journey from start to end.

If students get stuck, remind them of the five *W*'s: who, what, where, when, and why and how. By asking the question of each object, they should discover new "think links."

> "I invent because I cannot help it . . . I am an inspirational inventor. I get a complete picture in my mind of what the invention will be like when it's finished. . . . Inventing is really easy; it's the development work that's heartbreaking."
>
> —*Beulah Louise Patrick*

DISCUSS: What is "inspiration"? Why is it important to inventors?

Extension

Fill a box with miscellaneous objects. Pull out two objects at random, hold them up, and ask students for "think links." After making several pairs, challenge students to join each pair into an invention. For example, putting a compass on a ruler produces a measuring device for both direction and distance.

The Bonnet Boom

In 1798 Mary Kies invented a new way to braid straw into bonnets. Her invention quickly became an American craze. Sewing circles switched to straw braiding. Children braided straw at school. Straw bonnets even became "currency" for barter and trade at a time when coins were scarce.

Many so-called straw towns in New England grew rich selling Mary Kies's invention. Thousands of women had jobs for the first time in their lives. First lady Dolley Madison praised Mary Kies for all of these amazing successes.

Think Creatively!

Sure, an egg carton holds 12 eggs.
But think creatively! An egg carton could also be a . . .

- ◆ planter for growing seedlings
- ◆ watercolor paint mixer
- ◆ cash drawer for coins
- ◆ living unit for a model space colony

- ◆ sorter for screws and bolts
- ◆ funky ice cube tray
- ◆ sand castle mold
- ◆ base for a dried flower arrangement

Pick one of the objects above. Brainstorm eight creative uses for it.

1. _____

2. _____

3. _____

4. _____

5. _____

6. _____

7. _____

8. _____

Think Links

Finding links between two different objects is fun. For example, how is a magazine like a bicycle? Use your imagination, and you'll think of lots of links:

◆ Both are usually used while sitting down.　　◆ Both come in many shapes and sizes.

◆ Both take you on a journey from start to end.　　◆ Both give people pleasure.

Try it! Think of at least one link for each pair of objects below. Some are obvious. Others are a little more challenging.

1. How is a bowling ball like Swiss cheese? _____

_____

2. How is a mailbox like a bird's nest? _____

_____

3. How is a carpet like an orange peel? _____

_____

4. How are you like a computer? _____

_____

5. How is your circulatory system like a bus system? _____

_____

6. How is a sand castle like a stuffed *Stegosaurus*? _____

_____

7. How is the moon like a pizza? _____

_____

8. How is a football stadium like an anthill? _____

_____

💡 **Inventor's Challenge:** **Turn one of your links into an idea for an invention. Example: Like an anthill, a Fun-and-Games Stadium has thousands of tunnels and chambers. It's ideal for playing large-scale versions of games like hide-and-seek.**

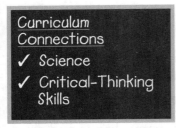

Rube Goldberg Machine-o-Matic

Students arrange a series of machine parts into an automated pizza deliverer.

Background

The essence of elegant engineering is creating a machine that does more with less. The fewer the parts, and the more work the machine does, the better the design. In the early 20th century, Rube Goldberg challenged that principle by drawing elaborate machines with many, many parts that did very simple tasks such as water the plants. Like the fictional Uncle Dan the Inventor, Goldberg's goal wasn't to create anything practical or useful. He used his imagination to play by drawing amusing cartoons that gently spoofed the process of inventing. In this sense, play (or tinkering) is an important part of the invention process.

Lesson Ideas

Divide students into teams for this cooperative activity. The cards on reproducible page 77 can be combined and rearranged in infinite ways, especially given the two blank cards on which students can draw any item they like. For example, here's an automatic lift for mounting an elephant:

1. Jump up on the trampoline.

2. Take the balloon from the monkey on the trapeze.

3. The balloon pulls you up to the kite.

4. Grab onto the kite.

5. Fly over to the elephant and land on its back.

The only rule for creating a pizza deliverer is to show or draw clear connections between each machine part—a clear cause and effect. The more cards each team can use, the better. Once teams know what they want to do, have them paste cards onto poster board and draw in connecting parts such as pulleys, a strong wing, a dotted line to show a trajectory, etc. Students should number and label each step of their machine. Adding sound effects in cartoon bubbles is a fun embellishment.

💡 Extension

Inventions by Rube Goldberg (Stewart Tabori & Chang, 1996) and other collections of the cartoonist's long-winded machines are readily available in most libraries. Using the books for reference, choose a machine and copy each part onto a separate card. Then challenge students to put the parts back in order.

Rube Goldberg Machine-o-Matic

Rube Goldberg invented machines that work too hard. These machines are designed to do simple tasks, yet they have many parts.

Cut out the cards below. Then, on another piece of paper, arrange as many of the parts as you can into a new machine. Draw and label the steps and any connecting parts needed to make your machine work. The purpose of your machine is to deliver a pizza to yourself.

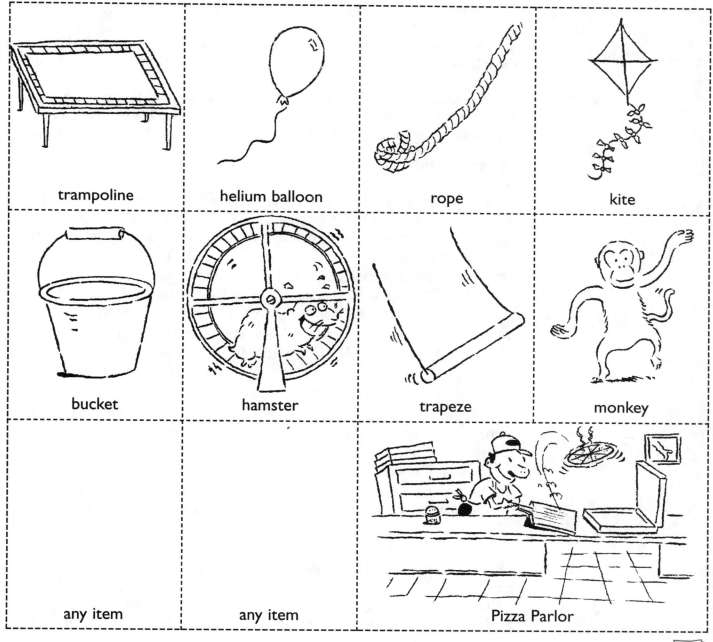

trampoline

helium balloon

rope

kite

bucket

hamster

trapeze

monkey

any item

any item

Pizza Parlor

Bag It!

Students examine how paper bags are constructed and then build their own models designed to hold as much weight as possible.

Background

Forget futuristic robots or souped-up space vehicles. By far, most inventions are part of our daily life. The more mundane, it seems, the greater the number of patents. There are thousands of patents for the mousetrap, the sewing machine, the bicycle, the can opener, the back-scratcher, and the paper bag!

Inventor Margaret Knight didn't create her paper bag overnight. Before applying for a patent, she rejected many designs, discarded many models, and sought expertise from many people. What kept her going? Each model improved the last. As inventors grow closer to their goal, they often become obsessed with "getting it right."

Perseverance and fulfilling a need are just two lessons to learn from Margaret Knight. She started inventing as a child and didn't let her age or gender stop her. At age 10, Knight invented a safety device for textile machines.

Lesson Ideas

Divide students into teams and hand out reproducible page 79. The goal isn't for students to make the perfect paper bag—it's to help them understand the invention process. Each step of the activity is important, and the final invention is much less relevant than the discoveries, mistakes, and thinking processes that go on beforehand.

Step 1: Why are grocery bags pleated? Why are bags made of different types of paper? Why do grocery bags have rectangular bottoms and other bags don't? Why don't all bags have handles? Is the paper uniform in thickness?

Step 2: How many pieces of paper does it take to make a bag? What is the weakest part of a bag? Which part gets the most abuse?

Step 3: Remind students that it's okay to change their design midstream. As they begin to build the bag, they'll see why.

Step 4: Make sure the tests are as uniform as possible, including where to hold the bag and how to add the marbles. Discuss volume versus strength: Is it better for a bag to hold a lot of marbles and risk breaking or to hold a few marbles with no possibility of error?

Step 5: Remind students that the invention process is never done. Even if they were to manufacture their bag, someone else might come along and improve it.

💡 Extensions

For a more open-ended challenge, add variables to the list in step 2 such as the type of material (string, plastic), and fasteners (staples, Velcro). Or challenge students to build a bag that uses as few materials as possible—and thus would be cheaper to manufacture—but that can still hold a certain number of marbles.

Bag It!

The paper bag seems simple. But it wasn't simple to invent. In the late 19th century, inventor Margaret Knight made model after model. After much sweat and failure, one bag finally worked. You are about to follow in Margaret Knight's footsteps. Can you build a super-strong paper bag?

What You Need (per team):
several paper bags (lunch bag, grocery bag, flat bag)
◆ scissors ◆ marbles or other weights

1. Study the paper bags. Gently take them apart. List all observations.

   What makes them strong? _____

   _____

   What special features do they have? _____

   _____

   What do these features do? _____

   _____

   Why are they built the way they are? _____

   _____

2. Brainstorm: What makes a paper bag strong? Write your ideas about:

   size (height, width, and depth) _____

   shape (flat, round, rectangular, cone-shaped) _____

   cuts and folds (where, how many) _____

3. On the back of this page, draw a sketch of your bag design.
   Label the features. Then make a model.

4. How many weights can your bag hold? (Hold the top and lift the bag.) _____

5. List three ways to improve your bag. _____

   _____

   _____

Cereal Science

Students experiment with cereal ingredients to determine how cereal makers invent new recipes.

Curriculum Connections
✓ Social Studies
✓ Science
✓ Creative Thinking

Background

Cereal making is highly scientific. Not any old ingredients will work together. Some won't work at all. And not every ingredient is what it seems to be. Physicists experiment with how bits of cereal mix, mesh, float, and sink—the science of granular substances. Biologists concern themselves with spoilage and sogginess. Chemists worry about dyes that run and how to simulate substances that are too expensive or delicate to include.

Here are a few examples of cereal science in action:

◆ Bits are generally the same size so that small ones won't drop to the bottom.

◆ Apples turn brown and so need special preservatives.

◆ Raisins clump together and so often have special coatings.

◆ All the ingredients must float the same way in milk so that they don't separate—some floating to the top and others sinking to the bottom.

◆ Consumers hate soggy cereal or lots of broken bits on the bottom of the box. Reducing sogginess and broken bits is an ongoing challenge.

◆ Peaches are too expensive, and so cereal makers substitute apples and add "peach flavoring." They can still use the term "peach" in the cereal name.

◆ Children like cereal that's fun. Machines called extruders work like cookie presses to churn out various fun-shaped bits with ease.

◆ The waxed bag inside the box keeps cereal fresher longer.

Lesson Ideas

At the grocery store, challenge students to find a cereal with raisins that doesn't have flakes. A few granola-type cereals include raisins and other dried fruits (cherries, strawberries, and so on); most of them have flakes, but a few do not. An interesting experiment is to compare the percentage of raisins that fall to the bottom. Have students do the activity on reproducible page 82.

Ask students to note the ingredients of other cereals. Do they observe any patterns? How many main ingredients do most cereals have? In their personal experience, which cereals hold up best in milk? Which have fewer broken bits on the bottom? What else do they like or not like about cereals?

All of this information is useful to know before inventing a brand-new cereal. You might want to hold a contest to design the best-tasting cereal (as tasted by a panel of impartial judges), the most economical one that still rates high in taste tests, or the most nutritious one.

Note: As students experiment, they may find that the data aren't always clear-cut. For example, raisins may stay mixed in a nonflake cereal if they are shaken one way but not another. Encourage students to replicate (repeat) their results. Also, you might want to redo the experiment using simpler objects such as various-sized marbles and sand.

💡 Extension

If possible, tour a cereal factory or write to cereal manufacturers such as Kellogg's, Post, and General Mills and ask for information about the machines and steps involved in the production of cereals.

This lesson was adapted from the November/December 1990 issue of *SuperScience Blue* magazine (Scholastic Inc.).

Cereal Science

Cereal makers almost always mix raisins with flakes.
Not "krispies." Not "O's." Not "mini-wheats." Just flakes.
Can you guess why? List a possible reason:

_____

Now do what cereal makers do: Experiment!
You can use the science you learn to invent your own cereal!

What to Do

1. Mix ½ cup (125 mL) of raisins and ½ cup (125 mL) of flakes in the container. Stir well with your finger to mix the ingredients.

2. Tighten the lid. Shake the container straight up and down 20 times.

3. Record your results below. Are the ingredients still well mixed? Or did one fall to the bottom? Did a lot of pieces break? What else do you observe? Repeat steps 1 to 3 for the other two cereals.

Flakes and Raisins: _____

_____

O's and Raisins: _____

_____

Squares and Raisins: _____

_____

Conclusion

What differences did you observe in the three mixes? _____

_____

_____

_____

Hypothesize

What is the reason for these differences? How could you test your hypothesis?
Write your ideas on the back of this page.

> ### Materials
> Clear, tall container with a lid
>
> Measuring cup
>
> 1½ cups (375 mL) raisins
>
> ½ cup (125 mL) each of single-ingredient cereals:
> - cornflakes or other "flake" cereal
> - Cheerios™, Froot Loops™, or other O-shaped cereal
> - Corn Chex™, Frosted Mini-Wheats™, or other "square" cereal

Join the BIRDS

Teams of students invent solutions to an iceberg collision, a sky-high rain forest study, an oil spill, and deadly space junk.

Background

The infamous *Titanic* tragedy spurred inventors of the day to devise iceberg-warning devices. Sir Hiram Maxim created a sonar device that sent out pulses too low for people to hear. The pulses bounced off objects and returned, setting off an alarm if an iceberg was dead ahead. Sound is only one possible way to detect an iceberg. Touch, radio or infrared light (as in remote control devices), trained sea animals, and satellites are a few inventive ideas. Here are a few other innovative solutions to modern-day challenges:

◆ Scientists now use a variety of vehicles and tools to explore the species that live in the rain forest canopy. A floating raft, a hot-air balloon, elaborate systems of pulleys and ropes, and suspension bridges are just a few devices.

◆ The *Exxon Valdez* accident in 1989 brought attention to an underestimated problem. Preventing oil spills with double hulls and the like was one area of focus. The other challenge was to clean up the spill without doing even more damage. Certain microbes eat oil, soap breaks it up, booms corral it into smaller spaces, high-power hoses wash down oily rocks, and so on.

◆ Space junk is a very real danger for astronauts in orbit. Billions of bits of old equipment could seriously damage a space shuttle's heat shields. Inventors have proposed a huge umbrella to catch the debris, an onboard laser blaster to destroy it, and higher orbits for all future spacecrafts.

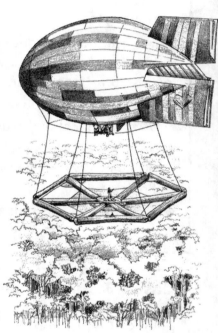

Lesson Ideas

All of these situations are complex, but the simplest ideas often lead to the best solutions. Divide the class into groups of four students and explain that students are members of a squad called BIRDS (Brainy Invention Rescue & Disaster Squad). BIRDS members save lives and the environment with brains, not brawn or bullets. Ask each group to read reproducible page 84, select a problem to solve, and assign roles:

◆ A researcher finds information.

◆ A recorder keeps careful records to put in a final proposal.

◆ A designer draws or builds models and sets up experiments.

◆ A leader coordinates efforts and runs brainstorming sessions.

The final proposal should include a restatement of the situation, a list of obstacles to overcome, data from experiments or research, a drawing (or model) and description of the group's best idea, and an explanation of why it is the best.

💡 Extension

Other problems abound. Scour the news for exciting challenges such as a proposed Mars colony in the 21st century, an underwater farm, and others.

Join the BIRDS*

*Brainy Invention Rescue & Disaster Squad

Your Mission (choose one):

Case #1: Berg Alert

In 1912 a brand-new ship called the *Titanic* hit an iceberg. Within hours, the huge ocean liner sank. Immediately, inventors set out to invent an iceberg-warning system.

The goal: Invent a device to sense icebergs and send out a warning in time for a ship to steer clear.

Tips:
◆ 90% of an iceberg is under water.
◆ Your Berg Alert should work from 900 feet (274 m) away (three football fields).
◆ Consider all five senses—sight, sound, touch, taste, and smell.

Case #2: Space Junket

In space, pieces of junk or debris fly at super-fast speeds. Even grain-sized specks can damage a spacecraft or a spacesuit. NASA has studied many plans for cleaning up this space junk.

The goal: Invent a device to collect or clear away junk in orbit.

Tips:
◆ Almost all of the junk is artificial—metal rocket and spacecraft parts, for example.
◆ It travels about 23,000 miles (36,800 km) per hour in low Earth orbit. At that speed, a marble would have the impact of a 400-pound (181-kg) motorcycle going 50 miles (80 km) per hour.
◆ What works to clean up junk on Earth—the bottoms of polluted lakes, for example?

Case #3: Slick Picker-Upper

Each year oil tanker accidents cause millions of gallons of oil to pour into the sea. To save ocean wildlife, clean-up crews have to get rid of the oil as fast as possible. Inventors have invented dozens of devices to get the job done.

The goal: Invent a way to remove, destroy, or reduce the effects of spilled oil.

Tips:
◆ Oil floats and spreads out in a thin layer on the water's surface.
◆ Later, globs of oil sink and smother life on the seafloor.
◆ To experiment, add a few drops of motor oil to a bowl of water.

Case #4: Treetop Transport

In the 1980s, rain forest scientists rushed to find new species of plants and animals. Most life forms live in the canopy (the high, windy treetops). So inventors had to invent a way to explore 100 feet (30 m) above ground.

The goal: Invent a device to allow scientists to move around easily in the high treetops.

Tips:
◆ Picture the canopy as a mass of thick, overlapping umbrellas.
◆ The rain forest floor (the "handle" part) is open and airy.
◆ Many animals get around the canopy just fine. How do *they* do it?

What's in a Name?

Students brainstorm names for inventions and analyze why some names are more successful than others.

Background

George Eastman, the inventor of the Kodak™ camera, said, "A name should be short, vigorous, and incapable of being misspelled." He liked the *k*'s in Kodak and so went with it. It also sounded a little bit like a shutter clicking. There are no hard-and-fast rules for naming a product. But there are most definitely categories of names to consider:

◆ Catchy names that create an image: Neon™, Apple™, Java™, Yahoo!™

◆ Descriptive names that tell what the invention does or what's in it: Formica™, Microsoft™, Pet Rock™

◆ Names targeted to a special audience: Stetson™ cologne, Buick Regal™, Gameboy™

◆ Personal and proper names: Ben & Jerry's™, Betty Crocker™, Sara Lee™

◆ Celebrity names: Air Jordan™

◆ Initials or acronyms: IBM™, NASA

Lesson Ideas

The audio toothbrush never made its maker wealthy and, though no one can say for sure, the blame may be in the name. "Audio toothbrush" just doesn't jump up and say, "buy me." Yet the product itself sounds entertaining. Have students complete reproducible page 86 to see what improved names they can generate—the more the better.

💡 Extensions

One study found that good names have several popular first letters in common: *S, C, M, P, B, A, T.* Is it true? Have students research product names and look for patterns and similarities. Perfumes, colognes, and cars are especially ripe for research. Is there an average length? How many words should a product name have? How many use alliteration—Coca-Cola™, for example? Have students classify the names into the groups listed under "Background" above. Do any new categories seem appropriate?

In 1989 an inventor named Gerfried Bauer created a similar singing toothbrush. His device has a tiny computer chip that could be programmed to play any song for two minutes—the time that dentists recommend people spend brushing their teeth. Divide the class into small groups and direct them to think of other toothbrush improvements and enhancements.

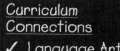

What's in a Name?

Ford Motor Company named one of its new cars Nova™.
Nova means "new" in Latin. The car did well in the
United States, but it flopped in Latin America.
In Spanish, *Nova* means "doesn't go"!

An inventor got rich selling ordinary rocks. How?
He called them Pet Rocks™. The rocks became a fad.

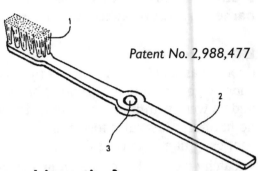

Patent No. 2,988,477

A name can make or break an invention. Can you name this real invention?

1. The toothbrush makes a nice sound while you brush. What three adjectives best describe this

   invention? _____

2. What does the toothbrush most remind you of? _____

   _____

3. List at least five similar words under each word below: *sound* and *music*, for example.
   Use a dictionary or thesaurus.

Sound	**Tooth, Brush, or Toothbrush**
_____	_____
_____	_____
_____	_____
_____	_____
_____	_____

4. Pair up words from the first list with words from the second list: *musitooth*, for example.

   Sound out the new words. Then write the best ones. _____

   _____

5. What would you call this invention? _____

Challenge: Create an advertising slogan or jingle for this product.

To Market, to Market

Students conduct a market survey on one of two levels of difficulty to determine public response to an invention.

Curriculum Connections
✓ Social Studies
✓ Language Arts
✓ Math

Background

All companies do market surveys, either formal or informal. Formal surveys are scientifically controlled. Informal surveys may be as simple as asking questions of friends and families.

The data from these surveys can't determine if a product will succeed. Rather, the surveys produce hard evidence of what is *likely* to happen when the product is released to the general public. They can also alert manufacturers to problem areas—an unpopular color, a weak name, and even an unintended use for the product.

Lesson Ideas

Remind students of the five *W*'s of a newspaper article—who, when, where, what, and why. These same questions can help shape a market survey. Who will buy this product? When is the best time to release it? Where is the biggest potential market? What do consumers like and not like? Why will consumers buy the product?

The hat on reproducible page 88 is a made-up invention. Use some of the brainstorming and thinking techniques presented earlier in the chapter to encourage students to design their own hat. The survey questions are just suggestions. Students can add or change questions to suit their invention.

The water toy on reproducible page 89 is an actual 1989 patent for a swimming aid. Would this invention be popular today? Are there other similar inventions around?

Have students graph the results of their survey to see at a glance how the data shape up. They should then prepare a recommendation report to the president of the company.

Patent Number 4,832,631 was invented to aid beginning swimmers.

💡 Extension

Here are some topics around which students can design their own survey:

◆ You want to design a new sneaker. Which styles are most popular?

◆ You have invented a new flavor of popsicle. Will people like it?

◆ You designed a board game. What should you call it?

◆ You created a walking stick that doubles as a horn for warning off motorists. What type of person would use this device?

Cap for Sale

You run a hat company called Heads Up! You have made every type of hat that exists. Now you want to try something new. For example, the hat at right gives people "eyes" in the back of their heads.

Cut out this hat and paste it on another piece of paper. Or draw a hat design of your own. Then survey people to see if they would buy it.

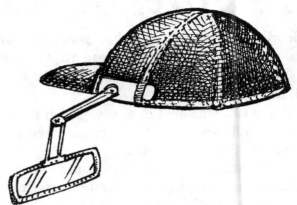

Question 1
Give your hat three possible names. Which name do people like best?

1. _____

2. _____

3. _____

Question 2
Find pictures of two popular hats in old magazines. Cut them out and paste them on the piece of paper next to your hat. Which ones would people want to buy the most? Ask them to rank the hats from 1 (most) to 4 (least).

Hat 1 _____

Hat 2 _____

Hat 3 _____

Question 3
On a scale of 1 (low) to 10 (high), how likely would people be to buy your hat? _____

Question 4
What do people like or not like about your hat?

_____

_____

_____

_____

Million-Dollar Question

An invention is useless if nobody needs it or wants it. That's why companies try to find out ahead of time if a product will sell. They conduct a market survey—a list of questions for people who might buy the product. You'll use a market survey to find out if a new water toy is worth a million bucks.

1. **OBJECTIVE.** State the goal of the survey— what you want to find out.

   Objective: To find out if you should invest $1 million in a new water toy.

2. **VARIABLES.** List factors that could affect sales.
   a. Price
   b. Competition (similar products)
   c. Popularity (whether people want it)
   d. Usefulness (whether people need it)
   e. Other: _____

3. **SURVEY.** Survey people at random about the sales variables (factors).
   a. About how much would you pay for the toy?
   b. Do you use similar toys? If so, what are they?
   c. On a scale of 1 (low) to 10 (high), rate the design. Rate the name. Rate how much you want to own this toy.
   d. On a scale of 1 to 10, how well can you swim? How often do you swim: daily, weekly, monthly, or less?

4. **DATA.** Compile and graph your data on a separate sheet of paper.

5. **DECISION.** Would you invest $1 million in this toy?

   ☐ Yes, because _____

   ☐ Yes, after making these changes: _____

   ☐ No, because _____

   ☐ I'm not sure. I want to know more about _____

   _____

   _____

The Money Game

Students calculate the cost of the parts in an invention and then determine the price that must be charged to make a profit.

Background

Not all inventors strike it rich. In fact, many inventors have patents for inventions that exist only on paper. One reason is cost. Besides the cost of the parts, inventors have to consider labor, marketing, advertising, overhead (such as office space), and much, much more. For that reason, few inventors manufacture their inventions themselves.

Lesson Ideas

Generate topics for a hot new board game. What types of parts will it have? How much will they cost? How much should the board game sell for? If students suggest low prices, such as $5, ask them if they think they'll make a profit. If their prices are too high, ask who they think will buy the game.

Reproducible page 91 shows students how to "crunch" the numbers. There's no correct answer, except to do the math accurately of course. Allow students to choose the size and number of games. Then discuss the various results.

Ask students to explain their decisions. Is a big game better than a small game? Do people believe that it's better? Discuss *perceived value:* how valuable a customer *thinks* a product is. Perceived value determines how much a customer will pay. For example, consumers tend to pay more for products that come in big, heavy packages. What about manufacturing costs? Why manufacture 5,000 versus 10,000 games?

Compare students' game specifications, including size and price. Which game would most people probably buy? Is the cheapest game the best game? What other factors determine the price? *(design, competition, size of market, willingness to earn lower profits or desire to earn more money, and so on)*

Answers

1. Small: $2.15; Medium: $2.40; Large: $2.65 2. 5,000: $2.10; 10,000: $1.60
3. Here are the possible variations: 5,000 small games: $4.25 cost and $21.25 price; 5,000 medium games: $4.50 cost and $22.50 price; 5,000 large games: $4.75 cost and $23.75 price; 10,000 small games: $3.75 cost and $18.75 price; 10,000 medium games: $4.00 cost and $20.00 price; 10,000 large games: $4.25 cost and $21.25 price.

💡 Extension

Posing as board game inventors, students must make a sales presentation to convince the Very Big Corporation to manufacture their latest game. Companies want hard data—like the numbers on the reproducible. But they also have to know who will want to buy the game and why it's better than the competition. Something as small as the name of the game counts!

SUBTOTAL 1: $2.40
SUBTOTAL 2: + $1.60
TOTAL UNIT COST: $4.00
× 5
PRICE PER UNIT: $20.00

SUBTOTAL 1: $2.15
SUBTOTAL 2: + $2.10
TOTAL UNIT COST: $4.25
× 5
PRICE PER UNIT: $21.25

SUBTOTAL 1: $2.65
SUBTOTAL 2: + $2.10
TOTAL UNIT COST: $4.75
× 5
PRICE PER UNIT: $23.75

SUBTOTAL 1: $2.15
SUBTOTAL 2: + $1.60
TOTAL UNIT COST: $3.75
× 5
PRICE PER UNIT: $18.75

The Money Game

Pretend you've invented a great new board game. How much will it cost to make? How much should you charge for it? Use a calculator to figure out the costs below. Then compute how much each game will cost.

1. Box and Board

Add the unit cost for each size: small, medium, and large. Then choose a size. Circle the subtotal for your chosen size.

Think: Besides cost, what are the pluses and minuses of each size?

	Small	Medium	Large
Box (each)	$1.25	$1.30	$1.45
Board (each)	$ .90	$1.10	$1.20
SUBTOTAL 1:	_____	_____	_____

2. Other Parts

Total each column. Then circle the subtotal for the number of games you choose to make.

Think: It takes less money to print 5,000 copies. There's also less risk of unsold copies. So why print 10,000 copies?

	If you buy 5,000	If you buy 10,000
Dice (pair)	$ .15	$ .10
Card Deck	$1.50	$1.25
Markers (4)	$ .30	$ .15
Manual	$ .15	$ .10
SUBTOTAL 2:	_____	_____

3. Total Cost and Unit Price

Add the two circled subtotals. Write the total in the blank for "Total Unit Cost." There are other costs to consider. These include creating the product, selling it, advertising it, shipping it, and more. To cover these costs, multiply your Total Unit Cost by 5 to find the price you must charge.

Think: Is your price too high? What choices can you change to lower it?

SUBTOTAL 1:		_____
SUBTOTAL 2:	+	_____
TOTAL UNIT COST:		_____
		x 5
PRICE PER UNIT:		_____

Parts of a Patent

Students learn to read and interpret a simple patent, including a technical illustration and persuasive prose.

Background

Patents were first legalized in England in 1624. The United States Patent Office opened in 1790. A patent is a legal document in which an inventor discloses all the details of his or her invention. In return, the government legally bans other parties from exploiting the invention. This ban expires after 14 to 20 years (depending on the type of patent) and applies only to the design specified. If the inventor improves the design, he or she must apply for a new patent.

Patents cost hundreds of dollars and can take months or even years to obtain. Not all inventions are patented. The makers of Coca-Cola™ declined to make public their secret formula, so other companies have not been able to copy it. Not all patent applications succeed either. An inventor has to persuade the Patent Office that the idea is new, useful, and not obvious (anyone could have done it). This persuasion takes the strictly formatted form of an illustration and an essay. It must be neat, well-thought-out, and detailed.

There are three types of patents: utility (mechanical or electric), design (appearance or style), and plant (crossbred flowers, and so on).

Lesson Ideas

Review the example of an actual patent on reproducible pages 93–94. Note that the patent is for an improvement of an original design. What's the improvement? *(studs and other devices to make the heel less slippery)* Would this patent be valuable today? Why or why not? Review the three types of patents and ask students to classify the boot heel. *(Utility—the design has a use and isn't just for looks.)*

💡 Extensions

Encourage curious students to research historical patents and choose one to present to the class. Several collections of patents may be available in your local library, among them:

◆ *Historical First Patents: The First United States Patent for Many Everyday Things* by Travis Brown (Scarecrow Press, 1994)

◆ *Historical Inventions on File*, an extensive loose-leaf collection (Facts on File, 1994)

◆ *Peculiar Patents: A Collection of Unusual and Interesting Inventions from the Files of the U.S. Patent Office* (Citadel Press, 1994)

Ask students to present classmates with the drawing part of an interesting patent and ask them to think about what the invention might be and how it might work. Their task is to complete the written part. How does the invention improve a task or situation? Who will use it?

Parts of a Patent

Two Rhode Islanders invented a reversible boot heel in 1868. When the heel wears out, just flip it upside down and use the other side.

Every patent has a number. More than four million patents have been awarded. This patent was awarded on July 4, 1871.

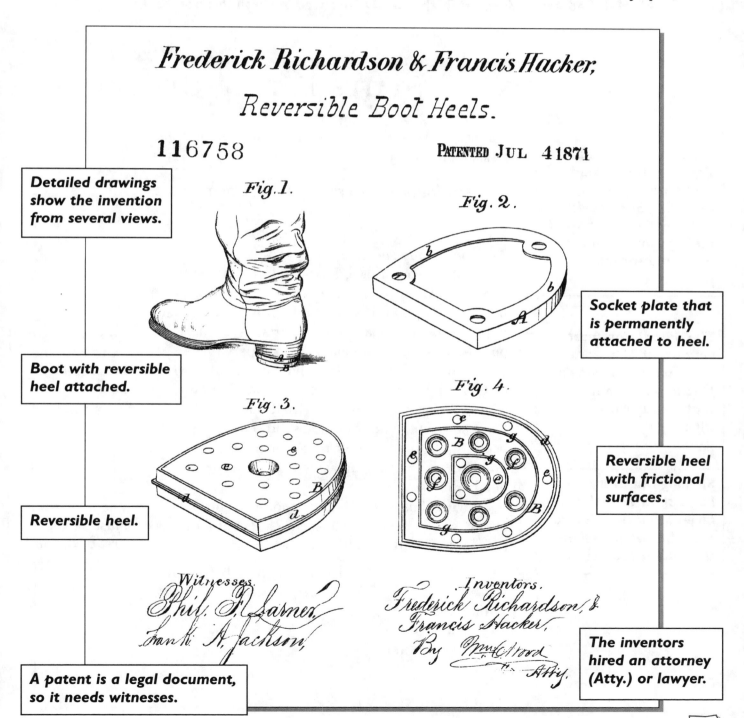

Frederick Richardson & Francis Hacker,

Reversible Boot Heels.

116758

PATENTED JUL 4 1871

Detailed drawings show the invention from several views.

Fig. 1.

Fig. 2.

Boot with reversible heel attached.

Socket plate that is permanently attached to heel.

Fig. 3.

Fig. 4.

Reversible heel.

Reversible heel with frictional surfaces.

Witnesses.
Phil. R. Sarner
Frank A. Jackson

Inventors.
Frederick Richardson, &
Francis Hacker,
By Wm. C. Wood
Atty.

A patent is a legal document, so it needs witnesses.

The inventors hired an attorney (Atty.) or lawyer.

Parts of a Patent

President George Washington created the Patent Office in 1790.
It grew from one person to a staff of thousands!

Look at this detailed essay describing the newly invented reversible boot heel.

116,758

UNITED STATES PATENT OFFICE

———

FREDERICK RICHARDSON AND FRANCIS HACKER, OF PROVIDENCE, R. I.,
ASSIGNORS TO "REVERSIBLE BOOT HEEL COMPANY," OF SAME PLACE.

———

IMPROVEMENT ON REVERSIBLE BOOT HEELS.

———

To whom it may concern:

Be it known that we, FREDERICK RICHARDSON and FRANCIS HACKER, have invented certain Improvements in Reversible Boot Heels. The Improvements consist in providing frictional metallic surfaces for the purpose of securing a foothold in slippery places.

For light boots, the reversible heel is filled with leather, rubber, wood, or other material. For ordinary winter use on heavy boots, the frictional spurs (marked e on the drawing) are solid. For miners' boots, studs (marked f) or ridges (marked g) are used. The heel may have spurs, studs, or ridges or any number of each.

Having thus described our improvements, we claim as new and desire to secure a Patent for the reversible metallic heel for the purposes stated.

FREDERICK RICHARDSON.
FRANCIS HACKER.

Witnesses:
HENRY MARTIN
JOHN C. PURKIS

The inventors already own a patent for reversible boot heels. But they have improved their invention enough to need a second patent.

The description must be very exact. The words are often technical. This phrase refers to metal that is rough, not slippery.

Spelling out every detail helps show how this invention is new. It also describes what designs the patent protects.

The essay must state how the invention will be used.

The invention must be the first of its kind.

Resources

For Students

About Inventions

The Book of Great Inventions by Chris Oxlade, Steve Parker, and Nigel Hawkes (Shooting Star Press, 1995)

811 Mistakes That Worked by Charlotte Foltz Jones (Doubleday, 1991)

Eureka! It's a Telephone and *Eureka! It's a Television* by Jeanne Bendick (Millbrook Press, 1993)

53 1/2 Things That Changed the World and Some That Didn't by Steve Parker (Millbrook Press, 1992)

The Flying Bedstead and Other Ingenious Inventions by Steve Parker (Kingfisher Books, 1995)

Guess Again: More Weird and Wacky Inventions by Jim Murphy (Bradbury, 1986)

Historic Tools and Gadgets by Bobbie Kalman (Crabtree, 1992)

Smithsonian Visual Timeline of Inventions: From the First Stone Tools to Satellites and Superconductors (Dorling Kindersley, 1994)

They All Laughed . . . From Light Bulbs to Lasers: The Fascinating Stories Behind Great Inventions That Have Changed Our Lives by Ira Flatow (HarperCollins, 1992)

What If? 50 Discoveries That Changed the World by Seli Groves and Dian Dincin Buchman (Scholastic, 1988)

What's Inside Great Inventions edited by Hilary Hockman (Dorling Kindersley, 1993)

About Inventors

Brainstorm! The Stories of 20 American Kid Inventors by Tom Tucker (Farrar, Straus and Giroux, 1995)

Girls & Young Women Inventing by Frances A. Karnes and Suzanne M. Bean (Free Spirit, 1995)

Outward Dreams: Black Inventors and Their Inventions by Jim Haskins (Walker, 1991)

The Picture History of Great Inventors by Gillian Clements (Knopf, 1994)

A Pocketful of Goobers: A Story About George Washington Carver by Barbara Mitchell (Carolrhoda, 1986)

The Real McCoy: The Life of an African-American Inventor by Wendy Towle (Scholastic, 1993)

The Unsung Heroes: Unheralded People Who Invented Famous Products (and other books in the series) by Nathan Aaseng (Lerner, 1989)

About Inventing

Experimenting With Inventions by Robert Gardner (Franklin Watts, 1990)

Inventions by Rube Goldberg (Stewart Tabori & Chang, 1996)

Looking Inside: Machines and Constructions by Paul Fleisher and Patricia A. Keeler (Atheneum, 1990)

Put a Fan in Your Hat! Inventions, Contraptions, and Gadgets Kids Can Build by Robert Carrow (McGraw-Hill, 1996)

Steven Caney's Invention Book by Steven Caney (Workman, 1985)

Time Machine: The American History Magazine for Kids (in partnership with the National Museum of American History/Smithsonian Institution)

Wheels at Work: Building and Experimenting with Models and Machines and many other creative project books, by Bernie Zubrowski (William Morrow, 1986)

Fiction

Applebaum's Garage by Karen Lynn Williams (Clarion, 1993)

Burton's Zoom Zoom Va-Rooom Machine by Dorothy Haas (Bradbury, 1990)

Dear Mr. Henshaw by Beverly Cleary (William Morrow, 1983)

The Fourth Grade Wizards by Barthe DeClements (Puffin, 1990)

The Gadget War by Betsy Duffey (Penguin, 1991)

New Kid on Spurwink Avenue by Michael Crowley (Little, Brown, 1992)

Professor Fergus Fahrenheit and His Wonderful Weather Machine by Candace Groth-Fleming (Simon & Schuster, 1994)

Tiny for a Day by Dick Gackenbach (Clarion, 1993)

For Teachers

Nonfiction and Reference

Ancient Inventions by Peter James and Nick Thorpe (Ballantine, 1994)

Feminine Ingenuity: Women and Invention in America by Anne L. Macdonald (Ballantine, 1992)

Great Inventions Through History and *Great Modern Inventions* by Gerald Messadiée (Chambers, 1991)

Mothers of Invention: From the Bra to the Bomb, Forgotten Women and Their Unforgettable Ideas by Ethlie Vare and Greg Ptacek (William Morrow, 1988)

Multimedia

How to Invent: A Text for Teachers and Students video or teaching guide by B. E. Schlesinger, Jr. (IFI/Plenum Data Corp., 1987)

Invention set of 3 videos (Smithsonian Institution and Discovery Channel, 1990). Fourteen short programs look at inventions from Leonardo da Vinci to the future.

Invention Dimension from the Massachusetts Institute of Technology (E-mail: invent@mit.edu). An internet resource for K–12 students, teachers, and others who want to learn about American inventors and their discoveries.

Invention Studio Mac/Windows/PC CD-ROM (Discovery Channel Multimedia, 1990). Includes lessons on brainstorming, keeping a journal, and a workshop for creating wacky machines.

Inventor Labs Mac/Windows CD-ROM (Houghton Mifflin, 1996). Offers three virtual labs to explore: Thomas Edison's, Alexander Graham Bell's, and James Watt's.

Organizations and Contests

Invent America! (1331 Pennsylvania Ave. NW, Suite 903, Washington, D.C. 20004) is an annual contest for grades K–8.

Inventure Place (221 S. Broadway St., Akron, Ohio 44308) conducts invention workshops and camps, publishes curriculum materials for schools, and sponsors the National Inventors Hall of Fame.

Odyssey of the Mind (OM Association, Inc., P.O. Box 27, Glassboro, New Jersey 08028) challenges teams of students in three divisions (grades K–5, 6–8, and 9–12) to creatively solve open-ended problems.

Project XL (Commissioner of Patents and Trademarks, Department of Commerce, Washington, D.C. 20231) aids and encourages teachers of young inventors through curriculum materials and a guide called *The Inventive Thinking Project*. Project XL and the Argonne National Laboratory (Energy and Environment Systems Divisions, Mail Stop 362-2B, Argonne, Illinois 60439) also distribute *Catalog of Junior Inventor Programs*.

U.S. Department of Commerce, Patent and Trademark Office. Write to the U.S. Government Printing Office (Superintendent of Documents, Washington, D.C. 20402) for pamphlets about patent history and how to file for a patent.

Women Inventors' Project (22 King St. South, Suite 500, Waterloo, Ontario N2J 1N8, Canada) is a nonprofit Canadian group that stages workshops and publishes information for girls and women interested in inventing.